THE BEST BAY AREA SPORTS ARGUMENTS

THE 100 MOST CONTROVERSIAL, DEBATABLE QUESTIONS FOR DIE-HARD FANS

CAM INMAN

Foreword by JOHN MADDEN

SOURCEBOOKS, INC.
NAPERVILLE, ILLINOIS

Published by Sourcebooks, Inc.
P.O. Box 4410, Naperville, Illinois 60567-4410
(630) 961-3900
Fax: (630) 961-2168
www.sourcebooks.com

Library of Congress Cataloging-in-Publication Data

Inman, Cam.
  The best Bay Area sports arguments : the 100 most controversial, debatable questions for die-hard fans / Cam Inman.
     p. cm.
  Includes index.
  1. Sports—California—San Francisco Bay Area—Miscellanea. I. Title.
GV584.C2I46 2008
796.097946—dc22
                            2008015972

Printed and bound in the United States of America
VP 10 9 8 7 6 5 4 3 2 1

CONTENTS

THE BEST BAY AREA SPORTS ARGUMENTS

THE BAY AREA'S SPORTS SUBURBS

Dedication:

To My Home Team: Jen, Kate, Brooke, and Grant.

FOREWORD

First of all, *The Best Bay Area Sports Arguments* is a great book.

If you're a contrarian like I am, when you read this you'll find yourself thinking, 'Well, is that guy better?' or 'That guy shouldn't be in there.' That's a great thing. It makes you think about whether you agree with the arguments: Is that the way you would go? Could you think of someone else? It brings out your spirit in an argument.

The other thing, it just brings you back to another time. It's going back over memories. Today, you read the news, and you read about the A's and Giants, and you think of today's A's and Giants. Then you go back and remember the other eras, like Reggie Jackson and Sal Bando and Billy Martin and that whole group.

Then there are the Raiders, and you think of the new Raiders and old Raiders. And you think of the 49ers back before the glory days, then their glory days and the whole Joe Montana–Steve Young deal. This book just makes you think of all those people.

And the basketball: I remember the Warriors, and how in the year we won the Super Bowl (with the 1976 Raiders), the Warriors also had just won (in 1975), and the A's had won their championships (from 1972–74). You talk about sports in the East Bay, and I don't know that it ever got any better.

This book puts everything in history in perspective. Sometimes today, we tend to forget our history, forget our roots and forget where things originated. History is not as important as it used to be. But I'm a big believer in that you can't know what is going on now, totally or thoroughly, if you don't know what went on before. To really know it, whatever it may be, you have to know the whole history of it. That used to be more important, for whatever reason, than it is now. We've got so much information at our fingertips, with computers and the Internet, we don't go back to see, 'Where did this start?' For example, does anyone remember Steve Young as a quarterback for the Tampa Bay Buccaneers when they didn't win a game, or when he was playing for the L.A. Express?

This book helps you get back to things like that. There's, 'Oh yeah, yeah, jeez, I forgot about that,' or, 'Oh yeah, yeah, I was there!' I love these kinds of things, and this book leads to discussions like that. There's a lot of wow factor, which I love.

This book is great idea for anyone to read, especially anyone in the Bay Area.

—John Madden

INTRODUCTION

I know what you're thinking: The Bay Area argues about sports? Who has time for that when we're busy admiring the Golden Gate Bridge at sunset, or heading to the beach on a blue-sky day, or packing for Lake Tahoe, or commuting on Highway 101, or getting the kids ready for soccer practice, or watching the dot.com industry fluctuate in Silicon Valley, or gauging our inflated yet plummeting home values?

Take it from a Bay Area native, I know sports' place in our society. When our teams are doing well, we all want a piece of the action. When they're not, as has been the dreadful case since 2002, we know we've got plenty of entertainment options to distract us.

This book will take you on a tour through the Bay Area sports scene's ups and downs. We will debate about the great ones who've played here: from Joe to Jerry, from Barry to Brandi, from Rickey to Reggie, from T.O. to Otto—along with the ones you may have forgotten—from Irbe to Uribe, from Sleepy to Campy, from Kezar Stadium to Seals Stadium.

In the 50 years since the Giants moved to San Francisco from New York, so many Bay Area teams have celebrated a championship at season's end. Well, most teams other than the Giants, that is. The A's had their 1970s dynasty, the 49ers had their run in the 1980s, the Warriors had Rick

Barry & Co., the Raiders had their "Team of the Decades" moniker and, yes, even Cal and Stanford produced titans on the gridiron and hardwood way back in the day. We'll talk about them all.

And, yes, Joe vs. Steve will be covered. It's the most obvious debate out there, or so it seems. That is, unless it's The Play that lifted Cal past Stanford in the 1982 Big Game, with Cal fans forever maintaining all five laterals were legal and no knees touched the turf. We've got the essential arguments like these, plus your standard dream teams and heroic home-run lists, of course, but we'll also throw some quirky questions into the mix, such as where's the Bay Area's best seat and who's got the best nickname. Here, you'll receive barroom chatter that goes far beyond the Giants or A's, 49ers or Raiders, Stanford or Cal, kayak or luxury box.

What you won't be is bored. You've endured enough of that watching various 49ers and Raiders offenses in recent years.

The goal here is to entertain, and yet educate. Writing this book taught me a ton about the Bay Area's storied sports history. Hopefully you'll find reading it just as informative.

Think of it, if you will, as a Bay Area sports encyclopedia that's fun yet enlightening. And know that it's not all my doing. So many colleagues, friends, and family helped in this process.

Yep, here comes the Emmy-esque, thank-you list. To my media brethren: Gary Peterson, Steve Corkran, Eric Gilmore, Mike Lefkow, Dave Belli, Tom Barnidge, Rick

Hurd, Jonathan Okanes, Marcus Thompson II, Joe Stiglich, Jon Becker, Ron Bergman, Ira Miller, Dennis Georgatos, Dan Brown, Mark Purdy, Tim Kawakami, Ann Killion, Lowell Cohn, Matt Maiocco, Phil Barber, Jeff Fletcher, Scott Ostler, Ray Ratto, Bruce Jenkins, Kevin Lynch, Glenn Schwarz, Henry Schulman, Glenn Dickey, Nick Peters, Art Spander, Matt Barrows, David White, Jerry McDonald, Geoff Lepper, Monte Poole, Carl Steward, Joe Fonzi, Joe Starkey, Rich Walcoff, Hal Ramey, Jim Barnett, John Cardinale, Mitch Stephens, Vince Golla, Demian Bulwa, Ed Vyeda, Raymond Ridder, Jim Young, Kirk Reynolds, and Brad Mangin.

To help balance out all those professional opinions (and surely others I've mistakenly omitted), I also called on my family (especially brothers-in-law), my friends (childhood chum Matt Bortner, the Rynos dugout, and my jerky college roommates), and anyone I happened to overhear while having a cold one at a bar near you.

I should also thank Al Gore, because the Internet was a great help, whether it came to researching old newspaper articles on Nexis or calling up favorite websites such as baseball-reference.com, or pro-football-reference.com along with assorted league and team pages. My editor, Shana Drehs, was a tremendous help, and let's give a shout out to her hubby, Wayne, who once taught me to never challenge a Michigan female boxing champ.

Of course, the biggest thanks goes to my immediate family—my wonderful wife, Jennifer, our darling daughters, Kate and Brooke, and our newborn son, Grant, who got his Huggies changed when I wasn't writing this book, if he was lucky.

So, which teams do I root for? Unfortunately, my objectivity came into play when I "turned pro" as a sportswriter at age 16. That's when, as a high school senior, I began getting paid for my prose by the *Cupertino Courier*, a weekly I used to deliver as a pup. Back then, I epitomized the Bay Area's front-running fan: From posters on my wall of 49er greats, to a mesh cap from a Raiders' Super Bowl title, to autographs from Giants All-Stars, to A's ticket stubs and "BillyBall" memorabilia, to chocolate malt lids at Stanford football games, to so much more. Somehow, over the years, I've managed to stash my tangible Bay Area sports memories into my garage rafters. Those past sports pages, magazines, and other paraphernalia actually came in handy when analyzing the ensuing debates.

Wherever this book ends up in your collection—be it the bookcase, the bathroom, or the backseat of your hybrid car—hopefully you enjoy it as much as you've enjoyed rooting for Bay Area sports over the years. At least back in the glory days.

Okay, time now for the greatest two words in sports: Play ball!

BEST OF THE BAY

JOE VS. STEVE: WHO DESERVED TO START IN THE BEST QB CONTROVERSY EVER?

1 No debate has riled the Bay Area more than Joe vs. Steve. It's the best quarterback controversy of all time, and it played out between two future Hall of Famers during the 49ers' dynasty in the late 1980s and early 1990s.

For the overwhelming majority of 49ers fans, there really wasn't much to debate. They wanted Joe Montana to forever quarterback the franchise he not only saved, but guided to its first four Super Bowl crowns. In the other corner was Steve Young, a left-hander initially known more for his knack of running wild.

In 1987, Young ran straight into 49ers lore, getting traded from the woeful Tampa Bay Buccaneers to the high-society 49ers. That didn't just give the 49ers a great one–two quarterback punch in Montana and Young. It also provided incessant water cooler chatter, even after Montana was traded away to the Kansas City Chiefs in 1993.

This debate didn't just rage for a day, a week, or a year. Heck, it's still rehashed today anytime Montana and Young are mentioned in the same breath. Seriously.

Considering how well the franchise fared, and how both Montana and Young are enshrined in Canton, you could argue that Joe vs. Steve played out well enough for all parties involved, aside from the icy relationship Montana and Young seemed to share, as well as the soap opera drama that accompanied their saga.

Montana is still quite beloved in the Bay Area sports scene. But Young has certainly made strides in the popularity department these past 20 years, especially with the insight he gives on both ESPN and his weekly radio show for San Francisco's KNBR 680-AM.

Montana took his place on the Bay Area pedestal after leading the 1981 and '84 teams to Super Bowl titles. Then injuries started to take their toll on him. Fearing that Montana's body might not respond well in 1987, 49ers Coach Bill Walsh brought in Young, and the best-ever QB controversy was born.

During his four-year stint as Montana's understudy, Young didn't happily stand idle, but he did gain tremendous knowledge. The quarterback controversy picked up steam at the end of that 1987 season, with Walsh pulling Montana in favor of Young during a 36–24 playoff loss to Minnesota. It was the only time Montana ever got benched for ineffectiveness.

Montana rebounded from elbow woes in 1988, and, although Young started the second game at New York, it was Montana who came to the rescue after halftime for a dramatic win against the host Giants. He went on to lead the 49ers to Super Bowl titles that season and again in 1989, so the debate certainly wasn't raging then.

Young finally got his chance as a full-time starter in 1991 and '92, as Montana battled a right elbow injury that required surgery. Young seized his opportunity and won NFL passing titles in both of those years, but losing the 1992 season's NFC Championship Game to Dallas at home meant that the fans still weren't convinced he was the best choice.

The ensuing offseason wasn't just Joe vs. Steve, it became Joe vs. the 49ers. Montana wanted a chance to win back his starting job in 1993 under Coach George Seifert. When all the 49ers offered was an 11th hour push by owner Eddie DeBartolo to name Montana the "designated starter" entering training camp, Montana requested a trade to the Chiefs.

This really served as the ultimate moment in the Joe vs. Steve debate. It was time to pick one or the other. Keeping both wouldn't work anymore, not after Young had proven himself as an elite quarterback in the 1991 and '92 seasons. Young had matured as a quarterback, grasped the West Coast system, and learned so much from Montana in their four years together. Young won only one Super Bowl in his ensuing seven seasons, but he kept the 49ers in playoff contention with staggering efficiency and excellent leadership.

Statistically, both Montana and Young put up heavy career numbers. Montana finished with three Super Bowl MVP honors, eight Pro Bowl trips, 40,551 passing yards, 273 touchdown passes, a 92.3 passer rating in the regular season and an astounding 127.8 Super Bowl passer rating. Young won six NFL passing titles (Montana won two), made seven Pro Bowl squads, passed for 33,124 yards, ran for 4,239 yards, was a two-time league MVP, and he won Super Bowl MVP honors for throwing six touchdown passes in the Super Bowl XXIX rout of San Diego.

Looking back on it all, Young faced tremendous pressure during his entire 49ers career, living in Montana's shadow. Yet Young became the first Hall of Famer to succeed another Hall of Famer, at any position.

We can thank both of them for giving the Bay Area one heck of a debate the past 20 twenty years. But, again, this really wasn't a debate as much as it was a soap opera. No one, not even a Hall of Fame understudy, could surpass Montana's magic. If you had to pick one or the other, you'd take Montana, based on his Super Bowl showings and clutch comebacks. The 49ers made the right call by sticking with him shortly after Young's arrival. And, as twisted as it sounds, the 49ers also made the correct move by dispatching Montana in the twilight of his career and letting Young take the throne in 1993. The debate had to end there—the time had come for Young to play, and the legacy Montana built was cemented for eternity.

WHO'S THE MOST REVERED ATHLETE IN BAY AREA SPORTS HISTORY?

2 Some of sports' greatest stars gained their fame playing for a Bay Area team. But when it comes to naming the Bay Area's most prestigious player, it seems obvious who should be recognized as number one no matter what side of the Bay you reside.

Let's look at the options first. We've got Willie Mays, Wilt Chamberlain, Bill Russell, Joe DiMaggio, Barry Bonds, Jerry Rice, Joe Montana, and Johnnie LeMaster, (just kidding on that one, Giants fans). All are worthy contenders, extremely worthy, in fact.

Mays is arguably the best baseball player ever to grace a diamond. It's just that most Bay Area fans under 40 can't relate to his playing days, outside of a black-and-white replay of his version of The Catch, which occurred in the 1954 World Series when he played for the New York Giants. Four years later, Mays and the Giants moved west to San Francisco, and yet Mays was still viewed more as a New York transplant than a San Francisco kid. Nevertheless, he continued his greatness here before getting traded in May 1972 to the New York Mets. He played 14 of his 22 seasons in San Francisco, where he also won 11 of his 12 Gold Gloves as well as the 1965 MVP Award. And keep in mind that Mays flourished despite often playing in the devilish winds at Candlestick Park.

Mays' overall brilliance notwithstanding, the Giants never won a World Series crown with him in San Francisco. The Giants did reach the 1962 World Series, but again, they've yet to deliver San Francisco a championship, either with Mays or with his godson, Barry Bonds.

Chamberlain's and Russell's dominance in the NBA is unmatched regarding their respective abilities to score at will, in Wilt's case, and win championships at a blistering pace, in Bill's case. Both made the Bay Area home for a while, but that's not where they made their biggest marks during sensational careers, a fatal blow to their candidacy in this debate. A product of Oakland's McClymonds High School, Russell led the University of San Francisco to NCAA titles in 1955 and '56 before becoming the Boston Celtics' centerpiece and winning 11 NBA titles in his 13-year career. Chamberlain played just two and a half seasons with the San Francisco Warriors before getting traded to Philadelphia's 76ers.

DiMaggio's Bay Area roots shouldn't be dismissed or forgotten. Born in 1914 in the East Bay port town of Martinez and raised in San Francisco, he played a few years for the minor league San Francisco Seals before shipping out to the New York Yankees in 1936. Joltin' Joe was a three-time American League MVP, a two-time batting champ, and the guy who produced a 56-game hitting streak in 1941. If only he did all that here in the Bay Area, but alas, major league baseball wouldn't arrive until the Giants moved from New York's Polo Grounds in 1958, three years after DiMaggio's induction into Cooperstown.

Bonds also grew up in the Bay Area, and he rejuvenated a Giants franchise that was on the verge of moving to Florida. He rewrote the record book with his offensive prowess (see: all-time and single-season home-run lists). As despised as he is through much of the nation for his boorish behavior and alleged use of performance-enhancing drugs, the Bay Area certainly has embraced more than rejected him. That said, his tainted career isn't one we're willing to embrace as symbolic of what we want out of the Bay Area's ultimate icon.

As for Jerry Rice, he had the finest career of any wide receiver, setting a plethora of records and winning three Super Bowls with the 49ers. From 16 landmark years with the 49ers, to another Super Bowl appearance with the cross-bay Raiders, to his final catches as a Seattle Seahawk, to a final training camp with the 2005 Denver Broncos, the hard-working Rice was a reliable weapon, especially for Montana and Steve Young. The 49ers won two Super Bowls before Rice arrived on the scene, though, and thus, the Bay

Area had already devoted its love to the guy who quarterbacked the 49ers to their first Lombardi trophies.

And Joe Montana is, after all this, our obvious choice. Montana won four Super Bowl rings with the 49ers. The path to those four rings forever changed how that franchise, and, perhaps the Bay Area, is looked upon by outsiders. For that matter, those rings surely helped the Bay Area stick out its proverbial chest.

The last pick of the third round in the 1979 draft, Montana went out and won the Super Bowl in his first full season as the 49ers starting quarterback, a Cinderella campaign in 1981. Of the 6,123 passes Montana threw in his Hall of Fame career (including postseason stats), one specific pass carved the way for his and the 49ers' magical run. It was a high, arcing spiral toward the back of the end zone that Dwight Clark hauled in for The Catch to decide the 1981 season's NFC Championship Game against the Dallas Cowboys. Hello world, indeed.

Next up for Montana and the 49ers was the first of four Super Bowl titles they would claim as Team of the Decade. Not since the Oakland A's won three straight World Series from 1972–74 had the Bay Area seen such continued success. San Francisco sure hadn't seen it, and now it not only had a franchise to which it could devote its Tony Bennett-sized heart, it had a champion quarterback who became a comeback victory machine in Coach Bill Walsh's burgeoning West Coast offense.

Never was that uncanny, cool precision on display more than in Montana's third Super Bowl, a riveting comeback win over the Cincinnati Bengals in Super Bowl XXIII on Jan. 22, 1989, in Miami. It wasn't just that he led the 49ers on a Super Bowl-winning drive in the final minutes of that 20–16 victory. It was how he did it. During a timeout in a 92-yard drive, Joe Cool pointed out to the boys in the huddle that comedian/actor John Candy was in the stands. Montana capped the Hollywood ending with a 10-yard strike to John Taylor for a touchdown with 34 seconds remaining.

Before Montana left the 49ers in 1993 via trade to Kansas City—ending the tumultuous Joe vs. Steve debate that began with Young's arrival in a 1987 trade—he established a championship legacy that remains unmatched.

WHAT'S THE BAY AREA'S BEST RECORD-SETTING MOMENT?

3 Some of sports' greatest records were not only broken by Bay Area stars, but the feats were accomplished on their home turf or infield diamonds.

When Barry Bonds blasted home run number 756 high into the night sky at AT&T Park on August 7, 2007, the predictable crescendo of confetti, banners, and fireworks escorted him to the top of baseball's home-run chart.

The instant Washington Nationals pitcher Mike Bacsik's 1–0 offering got smashed toward the center-field bleachers, Bonds lifted his arms in celebration, as did the sellout crowd of AT&T Park, an eight-year-old jewel on the San Francisco Bay shoreline that's been spoiled with so many other Bonds blasts.

This one was different, of course, because no one had hit 756 home runs in major league history. It was also unique because this joyous occasion was soured by accusations that Bonds used performance-enhancing drugs to pass Hank Aaron's hallowed mark.

Nearly three and a half years after Bonds testified to a federal grand jury about unknowingly taking designer steroids—according to transcripts leaked to the San Francisco Chronicle and later made public with his 2007 federal indictment on perjury charges—Bonds grabbed a microphone and addressed his home fans. The 43-year-old, seven-time National League MVP stood alongside his godfather, Giants legend Willie Mays, and thanked the crowd for this moment that "means a lot to me." About an hour later, Bonds tersely told reporters: "This record is not tainted at all. At all. Period. You can say whatever you want."

You can say it was a bigger moment than when Bonds broke the single-season home run record six years earlier. He surpassed Mark McGwire's 1998 plateau by hitting his 71st home run on October 5 at AT&T Park against the Dodgers. It was a first-inning solo shot, and before souvenir vendors could sell off memorabilia commemorating number 71, Bonds went deep again in the third inning, another solo shot, and like the earlier one, this also came against Chan Ho Park.

Okay, so 756 was bigger, and it was a shot everyone anxiously waited all season—perhaps even all of Bonds' career—to see. Yet, when it happened, the dramatic flair wasn't overwhelming. Why? Probably because the Bay Area has seen not only other milestone homers by No. 25, but other record-breaking moments, and by athletes who weren't as nationally condemned as Bonds was.

Like the A's Rickey Henderson. Of the 1,406 stolen bases in Rickey Henderson's 25-year career, his 939th stands out above the rest because, with that, he passed Lou Brock as baseball's stolen base king. On May 1, 1991, he nabbed third base in the fourth inning of a 7–4 win over the New York Yankees at the Oakland Coliseum. But Rickey wasn't done there. Before the umpire could even signal him safe, Rickey pulled the base from its moorings. Rickey held it above Rickey's head with one hand while Rickey pumped his other fist in celebration. So began a nearly 10-minute on-field celebration, including congratulatory words from Brock before a very memorable boast from Rickey.

"Lou Brock was the symbol of great base stealing," Rickey told the crowd of 36,139. "But today I am the greatest of all time. Thank you." He then stretched his arms up to the sky and relished the moment.

A few hours later, Rickey's feat got overshadowed when 44-year-old Nolan Ryan threw his seventh career no-hitter, for the Texas Rangers in a win over the Toronto Blue Jays. And it's overshadowed on our list too.

The premier record-breaking moment came when Jerry Rice became the NFL's all-time touchdown leader. He did so to cap a three-touchdown game. He did it before a record home crowd of 68,032, along with a Monday Night Football audience. He did it against the Raiders, albeit the Los Angeles version and not the cross-bay neighbors from Oakland. And he, or at least his coaches, called his shot.

Rice's 127th touchdown—a 38-yard catch with four minutes, five seconds remaining—broke Jim Brown's

13

record in a 44–4 rout of the Raiders on September 5, 1994. Prior to that outburst, Rice had scored against every NFL team except the Raiders.

He actually thought he would finish that night in a tie with Brown. But then offensive coordinator Mike Shanahan phoned him from the upstairs booth and told him to get back in the game. Garbage time? Nope. Record-breaking time.

Rice already scored on a 69-yard touchdown catch and a 23-yard reverse when he returned to the field and made a leaping catch of Steve Young's underthrown pass for TD number 127. Rice was only 31 years old, just 10 seasons into a legendary 20-year career that produced 208 touchdowns.

Everyone knows just how hard Rice worked to establish that record, from running up a Peninsula hill to perfecting his artistry on the 49ers practice fields. His record chase wasn't clouded by a grand jury. He didn't boisterously deem himself the best ever after breaking the record. He rejoiced in the perfect moment, on the perfect stage.

4 For 10 seasons, John Madden served as the Raiders coach and earned himself a spot in the Pro Football Hall of Fame. That's when the nation first took notice of this energetic, boisterous fella. Since then, Madden has become a mega-star, winning Emmys for his 20-plus years as a sports broadcaster and lending his name and insight to the most popular sports video game ever—EA Sports' "Madden NFL Football."

All you need to do is say Madden and your mind fills with images of a frolicking, fast-talking, football-lovin' guy. And since football is America's favorite sport, Madden is its main messenger.

But is he the Bay Area's most nationally recognized icon?

Al Davis promoted Madden at age 32 to coach the Raiders, and while Davis' presence has loomed large on the NFL stage for over 40 years, the public sees him about as often as the Punxsutawney groundhog, with Davis popping out seemingly every winter to announce a coaching change.

Joe Montana's legacy looms the brightest in the Bay Area, but he tends to keep a low profile. He'll crisscross the nation and speak about the dangers of heart disease. He'll sit in the stands at his children's athletic events. He'll pop up in "Joe's Diner" in a NFL Network commercial. But he's more reclusive when it comes to the public spotlight.

Jerry Rice sure hasn't shied away from the public eye since his retirement from a record-setting football career. He won over a new segment of the population with his performance on ABC's *Dancing with the Stars* in 2005–06. He's also dabbled in broadcast media, be it satellite-radio sports talk for FOX or Sunday night sports shows for a Bay Area television station. And he's forging a new career by grooming college wide receivers before the NFL draft, including USC product Steve Smith and Cal's DeSean Jackson.

What about baseball players? Willie Mays' past is too long ago for our country's short attention span. Reggie Jackson and Mark McGwire broke in with the A's, but their legacies really grew elsewhere, Jackson establishing his "Mr. October" moniker with the New York Yankees and McGwire breaking the single-season homer mark with the St. Louis Cardinals (not to mention testifying so lamely on Capitol Hill).

Surely Barry Bonds, with his stature as baseball's all-time home-run king, is nationally recognized, right? Bonds' presence off the field is nearly non-existent, as corporate advertisers have distanced themselves from him. He's the anti-Madden, if you will.

Raised just south of San Francisco in San Mateo, Madden still calls the Bay Area home, residing in the quiet East Bay suburb of Pleasanton. But when his famous Madden Cruiser hauls him out of town (he notoriously avoids flying), he heads off to his second homes, to football stadiums from coast to coast.

A *Boom!* here and a *Boom!* there, and his voice is instantly recognized (or mimicked by comic Frank Caliendo.) His face, meanwhile, has popped up on television since those Raiders coaching days, highlighted by the 1976 team delivering the franchise its first of three Super Bowl wins.

He's entrenched as one of America's leading pitchmen, starting way back with those Miller Lite commercials ("Tastes great!...Less filling!") to the current crop of hardware, steakhouse, and, of course, video game ads.

Such national notoriety dwarfs that of other Bay Area icons, and arguably anyone in the country other than Tiger Woods and Michael Jordan.

WHAT'S THE BAY AREA'S ULTIMATE TEAM MOTTO?

5 You've probably got a favorite team motto, a catchphrase that fits the great times of a certain era. For example, Giants manager Roger Craig's two-word pep talk, "Humm Baby," echoed throughout the club's late-1980s revival.

Coincidentally, one of the most identifiable Bay Area slogans features a different type of baby talk, that being Raiders boss Al Davis' demand to: "Just win, baby!" It's one of several mantras associated with the Raiders, including "Commitment to Excellence," "The Greatness of the Raiders," "Team of the Decades," "Pride and Poise," and "The Will to Win." Raiders players also have their own motto: "Once a Raider, always a Raider."

The Raiders' next-door neighbor, the Golden State Warriors, adopted a fan's credo—"We Believe!"—and turned it into a rallying cry during their stirring 2007 playoff run. It started out as a grassroots campaign to inspire the Warriors, with season-ticket holder Paul Wong passing out cheer cards and making his own yellow T-shirts saying "We Believe Playoffs." It became such a defining facet to the Warriors' run that the team followed Wong's lead and handed out "We Believe!"

cards and T-shirts to fans at Oracle Arena during their first playoff appearance in 13 years. The sight of those 20,000 yellow shirts made Oracle look like a beehive, and that very loud buzz created quite the intimidating environment for the Dallas Mavericks and, to a lesser extent, the Utah Jazz.

Maybe it's just something about Oakland that breeds mottos. The A's have had their share, such as going from manager Billy Martin's entertaining style of "BillyBall" in the 1980s to general manager Billy Beane's savvy personnel approach of Moneyball, as was the title of Michael Lewis's 2003 book about the A's and Beane's methods.

"BillyBall" became a million-dollar promotional campaign in 1981, luring fans to watch Martin's wily base runners (see: Rickey Henderson) blend so well with quality pitching and home-run hitting. But after the A's plummeted a year later, "BillyBall" had run its course and Martin was fired.

As for "Moneyball," it revealed how the low-budget A's became a perennial playoff contender behind a unique front-office strategy. Beane emphasized previously over-looked stats, such as on-base percentage and slugging percentage instead of RBI and batting average.

While some in baseball circles scoffed at the "Moneyball" approach, one Bay Area team tried mimicking it, at least to an extent, as the 49ers dug deeper into statistical analysis regarding player personnel.

The 49ers didn't adopt that strategy enough to develop their own motto, for they already had one, "Rollin' with Nolan," based on the 2005 hiring of Coach Mike Nolan. A more appropriate motto might have been: "Losin' with Nolan," as the 49ers posted a losing record in each of his first three seasons. Or, perhaps, another could have been: "Just lose, baby!"

This brings us back to our winner, "Just win, baby," the slogan that truly encapsulates the passion and demand Al Davis has for the franchise he's called home for over 40 years. It's even the title of a biography of Davis.

When Art Shell was rehired in 2006 for his second stint as Raiders coach, he said at his introductory press conference: "There's history here and players have to understand what 'Commitment to Excellence' means. 'Just win, baby.' They laugh when Al says that, but there's meaning behind that."

It meant Shell would be fired shortly after the 2006 Raiders went a league-worst 2–14 in his encore effort. It meant that Davis would hire Lane Kiffin, who, at 31, became the youngest coach in modern NFL history.

The term became cemented in Raiders lore when Davis implored his team to "just win" during a pep talk before Super Bowl XVIII—a 38–9 win over the Washington Redskins by the 1983 Los Angeles Raiders. When Davis rehired Shell, he vowed that the Raiders would recapture their nastiness. But, in return, only their record continued to look nasty under Shell.

There's one more great thing about "Just win, baby!" It can go to the bench, rest, and not get overused.

And throughout all the Raiders' recent troubles, Davis' quest for victory hasn't changed one bit. He doesn't want his beloved team to show improvement. He demands victories. He wants to just win, baby.

WHAT'S THE TOP BAY AREA SPORTS CURSE?

6 The Bay Area has enjoyed several championship celebrations, but it sure seems there should have been more, considering the talented stars and oh-so-close seasons we've endured. When titles aren't produced, and once we're done condemning the coaches, owners and players, we might drift into fantasyland and think we're cursed.

We don't have a famously titled curse, like Chicago's Billy Goat or Boston's Bambino, the latter of which has been exorcised. But we do have plenty of contenders.

Let's look at Cal football, which, of all Bay Area teams, must be cursed. Just what that curse is, however, remains unknown. Cal hasn't won a national championship—or, specifically, finished atop a poll—since 1937. Seventy years later, the Bears were on the precipice of a number one national ranking, only to lose six of their final seven regular season games. Maybe we should call it the "Helmes and Dunkel Curse." Cal's 1937 "Thunder Team" finished atop only the Helms Foundation and Dunkel ratings while Pittsburgh took the top spot in eight other recognized polls, including the Associated Press's that debuted a year earlier.

Not every team has had such long-standing bad luck. With five Super Bowl trophies on display in their lobby, the 49ers wouldn't seem to be cursed. But they sure haven't done much since winning that last championship in the 1994 season, which brings us to the Curse of *Joe Millionaire*. Never heard of it? Here goes: The 49ers' rebuilding process had taken their 2002 team into the NFC playoffs. After a sensational comeback over the New York Giants in wild-card action, the 49ers went on to lose to the Tampa Bay Buccaneers. Team owner John York stood outside the 49ers locker room after that defeat and vowed to keep Steve Mariucci as his coach. A couple days later, while Mariucci was at home watching the television reality show *Joe Millionaire*, an irate York phoned him and summoned Mariucci to his office the next day. Word of Mariucci's firing broke that next morning on the radio while York was in his office dismissing Mooch. York admitted later he should have handled Mariucci's dismissal better. Ya think? The 49ers then reeled off five straight losing seasons, a streak they've never endured before in their 62-year history.

San Francisco's other fabled franchise sure seems like it's cursed, too. After all, the Giants haven't won a World Series title since moving to San Francisco 50 years ago. They've made it to that ultimate October stage three times, in 1962, 1989, and 2002. One moment in Giants infamy came in Game 6 of the 2002 World Series. The Giants were eight outs away from clinching the series against the Anaheim Angels when manager Dusty Baker made a fateful trip to the mound to take out Russ Ortiz. Before Ortiz headed for the dugout with a 5–0 lead intact, Baker gave him the ball as a souvenir. Felix Rodriguez took the mound and Scott Spiezio promptly belted a three-run homer. The Angels scored three more runs in the eighth, and the Giants lost 6–3. The Giants dropped Game 7, as well, and, voila, you've got the Curse of Dusty's Handoff.

But the top one in Bay Area sports lore is the Curse of Eddie Grant. He left the New York Giants, became a war hero, and had a plaque erected in his honor outside New York's Polo Grounds. When the Giants moved west, they didn't bring the plaque, and some trace that to the franchise's San Francisco failures. In 2006, the Giants eventually hung a replacement plaque in Grant's honor outside AT&T Park. But that still hasn't been enough to quell the curse. He wasn't the best ballplayer (he hit .208 in 1915, the final year of his career and only his second full season with the Giants), but his legacy taught us all a lesson: Respect your team's history, and whatever you do, pack up any and all monuments if you're skipping town.

WHICH PLAYERS HAD THE COOLEST NICKNAMES?

7 What's in a name? Well, a nickname, of course.

Here are our criteria to judge which is the best nickname: the winner must be snappy, unique, and so distinguishable that one mention of it and you know which player owns it. And while each Bay Area franchise features clever nicknames for individual players, there've also been monikers given to tag team partnerships or a franchise's style. Here are the top nicknames:

49ERS

In the category of best individual nickname, the winner is Bill "The Genius" Walsh. That beats out Hugh "The King" McElhenny, Jack "Hacksaw" Reynolds, Joe "The Jet" Perry, Joe "Joe Cool" Montana, Joe "The Comeback Kid" Montana, R.C. "Alley-Oop" Owens, Bob "The Geek" St. Clair, and Jerry "Flash 80/Fifi/J.R./World" Rice.

In category of group nickname, "Million Dollar Backfield" is tops, as that described the heralded 1950s backfield of John Henry Johnson, Joe Perry, Hugh McElhenny, and Y.A. Tittle. Another to consider: "Dwight Hicks and the Hot Licks," named after Hicks and his secondary mates, Ronnie Lott, Eric Wright, and Carlton Williamson.

RAIDERS

As tempting as it is to select "Al" or "Mr. Davis" as the premier nickname in Raiders history in honor of team icon Al Davis, the best true nickname belongs to Ken "The Snake" Stabler. That trumps Jim "Mr. Raider/Pops" Otto, Jack "The Assassin" Tatum, Ted "Mad Stork/Kick 'Em in the Head Ted" Hendricks, George "The Hitman" Atkinson, Daryle "The Mad Bomber" Lamonica, Skip "Dr. Death" Thomas, Fred "The Hammer" Williamson, and Dave "The Ghost" Casper.

The top group nickname goes to the "Soul Patrol," the hard-hitting defensive backfield of Tatum, Atkinson, Thomas, and Willie Brown. Let's also not forget "Highway 63 and 78," given to left guard Gene Upshaw and left tackle Art Shell. Recent teams have also received their share of nicknames, but considering kids might be reading this, we'll spare you some of the curse-filled monikers offered up by disgruntled fans.

A'S

Jim "Catfish" Hunter beats out Joe "Blue Moon" Odom (nicknames given to them by owner Charlie Finley). Simpler nicknames came with Mark "Big Mac" McGwire, Dennis "Eck" Eckersley, Roland "Rollie" Fingers, and Bert "Campy" Campaneris. The 1972 A's "Mustache Gang" takes top honors for group nickname, edging the "Bash Brothers" combo of Mark McGwire and Jose Canseco, as well as "The Three Aces" pitching trio of Mark Mulder, Tim Hudson, and Barry Zito.

GIANTS

Nobody comes close to Willie "The Say Hey Kid" Mays. Other candidates include Orlando "Cha Cha/The Baby Bull" Cepeda, Willie "Stretch" McCovey, Juan "The Dominican Dandy" Marichal, Greg "Moonman" Minton, Will "The Thrill" Clark, Rod "Shooter" Beck, Barry "Barroids" Bonds, Jeffrey "Hac-Man" Leonard, Jack "The Ripper" Clark, Charles "Chili" Davis, and Rick "Big Daddy" Reuschel.

There wasn't a more famous group of Giants than the 1963 "All-Alou" outfield of brothers Felipe, Matty, and Jesus.

WARRIORS

The eye-opening nickname here belongs to Eric "Sleepy" Floyd. Honorable mention goes to Wilt "The Stilt/The Big Dipper" Chamberlain, Baron "B-Diddy/Boom Dizzle" Davis, "Never Nervous" Purvis Short, Tyrone "Mugsy" Bogues, and Robert "The Chief" Parrish. Best group nickname goes to "Run TMC," that early 1990s trio of Tim Hardaway, Mitch Richmond, and Chris Mullin.

SHARKS

Hockey teams are on thin ice when it comes to quality nicknames, as few exist. But one of the all-time best goalie nicknames—and the Sharks' No. 1 moniker—belongs to Arturs "Like Wall" Irbe. The close runner-up for top nickname is "Pickles," which belongs to defenseman Marc-Edouard Vlasic. The catchiest nickname for a famous line is the "-Ov Line," in honor of Igor Larionov, Sergei Makarov, and Johan Garpenlov.

Okay, so which is the best nickname of that bunch? Well, here's a hint: It doesn't take a "genius" to figure it out. That's right, let's give the honor to the late Bill Walsh, "The Genius" who transformed the 49ers into a Super Bowl dynasty and left a lasting mark on the NFL with his clever schemes and innovative methods. Now that's a nickname that says it all about a man's talents, and it's not one thrown around lightly. As proud as he was of his accomplishments, though, Walsh probably would have preferred being known as "The Prankster," for his sense of humor made a lasting impression on those around him. Rest in peace, Genius.

WHAT'S THE BEST BAY AREA SPORTS ARTIFACT?

8 When it comes to Bay Area sports memorabilia, there's no shortage of famous artifacts fans would love to have. But here's one that won't—or, at least, shouldn't—turn up on eBay: "The Stanford Axe." Since 1933, The Axe has been awarded annually to the winner of the "Big Game," a matchup between Cal and Stanford's football teams dating back to the turn of the century.

The Axe is asterisk-free—unlike Barry Bonds' record-setting, home-run balls—and it's always under lock and key, so it won't ever get confused with an imitation ax. Plus, its rich history takes on a new chapter every year.

When Stanford reclaimed The Axe on December 1, 2007, after its five-year stay on the Berkeley campus, Cardinal fans celebrated for more than an hour inside their two-year-old stadium after upsetting Cal 20–13. Stanford students rushed the field immediately after the win and congregated around The Axe, which was introduced in 1899 at a pep rally before a Stanford-Cal baseball game.

Back then, Stanford students unveiled The Axe by using it to shred a blue-and-gold straw man, and after Cal won the baseball game the next day, Cal students stole (saved?) The Axe and cut off half its handle to smuggle it on to a Berkeley-bound ferry. It spent the next 30 years in a bank vault before the schools turned it into the Big Game's annual prize.

But what about the football that's so symbolic of the 49ers' 1980s dynasty? You know, the one Joe Montana threw for a touchdown to Dwight Clark. "The Catch" lifted the 1981 49ers past the Dallas Cowboys in the NFC Championship Game and paved the way for the 49ers' first Super Bowl win.

When Clark was asked in 2006 about the ball's whereabouts, he claimed it was in his closet. But is it the actual ball? After spiking "The Catch," Clark claimed the ball went to, fittingly, a ball boy, who then handed it off to assistant equipment manager Ted Walsh, who gave it to Clark in the locker room. Clark said he asked 49ers' public relations director Jerry Walker to hold on to the ball, and when Clark retrieved that ball, he displayed it in his restaurant before banishing it to a closet at home.

But there's a twist to Clark's story: After the Boston Red Sox won the 2004 World Series, ESPN did a segment on famous balls, and Clark said his "Catch" ball was in his closet. A couple weeks later, a report surfaced that the ball boy gave Clark an imposter ball and sold the original "Catch" ball for $50,000. Clark says he still thinks he has the right ball, but he can't be sure.

Just over 25 years after "The Catch," major league baseball dispatched an authenticator to put a secret stamp on the specialized baseballs used during Barry Bonds' 2007 pursuit of Hank Aaron's home-run record. When Bonds sent that record-breaking ball into the center-field bleachers in 2007, police whisked away the fan who caught it. That lucky guy was a New York tourist who promptly sold number 756 for $750,000 to New York fashion designer Marc Ecko. That ball's fate was then left up to the public, which decided in an Internet vote to brand the ball with an asterisk and send it to the Hall of Fame, thus reflecting the widespread perception that Bonds achieved the record by using performance-enhancing drugs. Bonds, after the season, claimed he would forever boycott the Hall of Fame if that ball showed up there first with an asterisk. Because of the controversy surrounding the ball—and perhaps the fact it got snatched by a New York tourist on a layover to Australia, and that it was sold to a New York millionaire—it's not a memento Bay Area fans are dying to embrace.

As for Bonds' 73rd home-run ball, the one that set the single-season record in 2001, a court battle ensued over which fan owned it. A judge ordered those two fans, Patrick Hayashi and Alex Popov, to sell the ball and split the proceeds. That ball's value (it sold for $450,000), along with so many other Bonds' blasts, might forever be tainted after his federal indictment on perjury charges regarding the use of performance-enhancing drugs.

Given the controversies and confusion, the choice is clear. We'll stick with The Axe as the Bay Area's ultimate sports memento.

9 Who doesn't love free stuff? One common way to lure sports fans into arenas is give-away days. You know the promotional schwag: bobblehead dolls, magnet schedules, duffle bags, blankets, caps, etc. The Giants once doled out trendy painter's caps in the 1980s with players' nicknames on them, such as "Moonman," "Chili," and "Blood."

All that's fine and dandy to stow away in your closet and garage. But give us something that truly shows loyalty, a reward for being there at the best and worst of times.

Okay, then here's the ultimate badge of honor: The Croix de Candlestick pin. Fans didn't just receive them; they earned them. The pins were awarded to fans at the conclusion of extra-inning games the Giants won on their home field, the windy and often chilly confines of Candlestick Park. Atop the orange pin is the "Croix de Candlestick" name, and on the bottom is "Veni Vidi Vixi," meaning "I came, I saw, I survived"--a play on Julius Caesar's words "Veni Vidi Vici" ("I came, I saw, I conquered"). The center of the pin is a snowcapped "SF" logo.

Up the shoreline closer to downtown San Francisco, fans still wear those relics on their caps or jackets when they visit the Giants' newer home, picturesque AT&T Park. The orange pins aren't much bigger than a thumbprint. But their meaning, their legacy is unmatched. So cherished is the "Croix de Candlestick" button that it came back to life in May 2008, albeit as a promotional giveway at a Giants game to celebrate the team's 50th anniversary in San Francisco.

The Golden State Warriors came pretty darn close to an equally charming fan freebie during their 2007 playoff run. That's when they gave away yellow T-shirts inscribed with that playoff run's motto: "WE BELIEVE!" Fans got a bonus gift, too: A yellow cheer card that also sported the "WE BELIEVE!" theme. If you saw how Oracle Arena resembled a beehive with all those yellow shirts and cards during the Warriors' historic first-round upset of the top-seeded Dallas Mavericks, then you, too, had to believe these fan freebies may have helped intimidate the Mavericks into taking so many bad shots, creating a yellow brick road, if you will. Although the yellow shirts returned for an unsuccessful second-round series against the Utah Jazz, the Warriors didn't try for another encore when they opened the 2007–08 season, and perhaps it's no coincidence they lacked a similar aura while losing their first four home games.

If fireworks displays count as a fan freebie, then hail the A's for their numerous shows over the years. But, um, you can't quite take home a firework, can you?

You can take home a football when it lands in your lap at a San Jose SaberCats arena-league game. Same goes for a hockey puck at a Sharks game. But, that, of course, entails going to HP Pavilion and actually watching hockey, a daunting task for some weary sports fans who might be more enticed to come by giving them, say, a Croix de Pavilion?

IS THE BAY AREA THE CAPITAL FOR SPORTS DOPING?

 Remember how reviled East Germany was for sending doped up athletes to sweep up Olympic medals? Well, the sports world has a new hub when it comes to performance-enhancing drugs, and, no, it's not whatever town the Tour de France is racing through in the summer.

The Bay Area is where it's at when it comes to steroid distributors and users, or perhaps you didn't hear about that little BALCO scandal that sparked a federal case and threatened to destroy Barry Bonds' legacy, not to mention those of other world-class athletes.

Up until the feds raided it in 2003, the Bay Area Laboratory Cooperative seemed like a harmless, one-story building on the San Francisco peninsula. However, BALCO founder Victor Conte helped distribute designer steroids that weren't supposed to be detectable by drug tests. Then the word got out. Conte, his suppliers, and fellow distributors went to jail. BALCO's touted clientele took a toll, too, such as track and field star Marion Jones forfeiting her five medals from the 2000 Olympics, and

Bonds getting indicted by the feds for perjury and obstruction of justice.

Bonds was part of a conga line of stars called in to testify before a federal grand jury, and his Nov. 15, 2007, indictment was based on his claims he did not knowingly take performance-enhancing drugs. That 2003 testimony, along with those of fellow baseball players Jason Giambi and Gary Sheffield and sprinter Tim Montgomery, were leaked to two San Francisco Chronicle reporters, Mark Fainaru-Wada and Lance Williams. The juicy details—or rather the "cream" and "clear" ones—from that leaked testimony were reported in 2004 by Fainaru-Wada and Williams, whose award-winning work led them to publish a bestselling book, Game of Shadows. Bonds' testimony was the star attraction, as he reportedly admitted taking a "clear" substance and a "cream" that were steroids designed to be undetectable. Bonds, according to grand jury transcripts, claimed he was told by his personal strength trainer—and childhood friend—Greg Anderson that the clear was flaxseed oil and that the cream was a rubbing balm for arthritis.

The BALCO case spurred Congressional hearings on performance-enhancing drugs in sports, and it led baseball to redo its steroid policy. In the wake of the 2005 release of Game of Shadows, baseball commissioner Bud Selig asked former Senate majority leader George Mitchell to investigate the use of steroids and performance-enhancing drugs in baseball.

When the Mitchell Report came out on December. 13, 2007, it delivered shock waves from coast to coast, and reporters in New York and Los Angeles claimed their region had been hit hardest. Silly them. No matter how damning the Mitchell Report's findings (or accusations) were in those cities, the Bay Area still stood as the true centerpiece of the Mitchell Report, thanks mainly to BALCO, Bonds, Mark McGwire, Jose Canseco, the Giants, and the A's.

That didn't stop a New York Daily News columnist from claiming "no team fared as badly, or as prominently, as the Yankees," who had 20 players from their 1999–2004 dynasty named in the Mitchell Report. New York, actually, had a couple other reasons to debate its case as a steroid haven, as much of the Mitchell Report's findings were based on testimony from New York Mets clubhouse employee Kirk Radomski and personal trainer Brian McNamee, whose clients included New York Yankees pitchers Roger Clemens and Andy Pettitte.

Florida also might want to argue its case as a performance-enhancing drug hotbed, as the Mitchell Report noted how some "rejuvenation clinics" were discovered to have supplied human growth hormones and steroids to athletes.

Across the country, a Los Angeles Times reporter claimed that "no team came off worse" in the Mitchell Report than the Dodgers. The basis of that claim: Team officials did not act on their suspicions that some star players were using steroids.

Sorry, but the Mitchell Report's ramifications hit home best in the Bay Area. It rehashed the BALCO scandal and it fingered a cadre of former Giants and A's, including Bonds and Giambi, who won MVP awards with the Giants and A's, respectively.

Other Giants named in the report were catchers Benito Santiago and Bobby Estalella; outfielders Glenallen Hill, Armando Rios, and Marvin Benard; infielders Matt Williams, David Bell, and Mark Carreon; and relievers Matt Herges, Jason Christiansen, and Mike Stanton.

The A's contingent in the report included McGwire, Canseco, 2002 American League MVP Miguel Tejada, Jason Giambi, Jeremy Giambi, Jose Guillen, David Justice, Cody McKay, Adam Piatt, F.P. Santangelo (a former Giant and Dodger), and Jack Cust, who was the lone active A's player in the Mitchell Report.

The Giants and A's front-office staffs also didn't come off looking swell in the Mitchell Report, which cited instances where team officials may have suspected steroid use among their players but did not report any findings to the league. The Giants brass, specifically owner Peter Magowan and General Manager Brian Sabean, took direct criticism in a follow-up Congressional hearing, as Selig was peppered with questions about the Giants' oversight regarding steroids, Bonds, and his shady trainer with BALCO links.

BALCO's impact also reached the NFL, when four players with Raiders (and BALCO) ties failed a drug test for a designer steroid, that fab four being Bill Romanowski, Dana Stubblefield, Chris Cooper, and Tyrone Wheatley. They were the first Bay Area football players suspended by the NFL for steroids since 1999, when 49ers kick returner Travis Jervey drew a four-game suspension.

Jervey's case went relatively under the radar, and it was the calm before the BALCO storm that's put the Bay Area at the forefront of the world's performance-enhancing drug scandals.

WHAT STADIUM IS THE MOST DANGEROUS?

This kind of argument may not come up in many cities across America, but here in the Bay Area we have a wealth of options.

Most would say that you haven't experienced danger at a sporting event until you plop down in Memorial Stadium's end zone bleachers at the University of California in Berkeley. A major earthquake fault runs under the stadium, from goal post to goal post. While a small crack is constantly creeping along, you never know when that Hayward Fault will wake up and possibly swallow Memorial Stadium's occupants.

That fault is projected to deliver the next great wallop to the Bay Area, registering as high as a magnitude 7.4. If, on the long shot chance it happens during one of Cal's home football games, it wouldn't be the first earthquake to interrupt a Bay Area sporting event, and we're not talking about the 5.6 jolt on the Richter scale that rattled Golden State Warriors fans at the 2007 season opener.

Think back to Game 3 of the 1989 World Series at Candlestick Park, when the 7.1 Loma Prieta quake rocked the region, collapsed roadways including part of the Bay Bridge and, for our purposes here, delayed what eventually became a four-game sweep by the Athletics over the Giants. Candlestick began hosting 49ers games 18 years earlier, and it still is to this day, despite the dismay of 49ers fans who are leery of that concrete relic. No one died at Candlestick during that 1989 World Series shake, but one fan did lose his life there during the 49ers' 2007 season, accidentally falling 20 feet from an upper-level walkway.

When it comes to danger, there's always the wrath fans can endure by wearing the uniforms of a hated rival to a Bay Area event. Think L.A. Dodger blue, K.C. Chiefs red and, when it comes to the Stanford-Cal "Big Game," either Cardinal red or Bears blue and gold, depending on the venue.

But you don't necessarily have to be dressed in the wrong colors to find danger at Oakland's McAfee Coliseum. As menacing as Raiders fans can be with their creative ensembles that include spikes, skulls and down-right scary face paint, don't necessarily lump all those passionate souls into the same category as the criminals who might turn the Coliseum into a shooting gallery.

Early in the 2007 season, gunshots rang out in the Coliseum parking lot. Four men were wounded as they tailgated the night before the game—the victims were mistaken as gang members, according to police reports—and another man was shot the following day after the Raiders' loss to the Chiefs. If only the Raiders' offense were as threatening as the outside elements on the mean streets of Oakland.

Unsportsmanlike conduct by fans isn't anything new there, or elsewhere in the Bay Area, as old 49ers players can attest. They often had beer bottles thrown at them as they walked off the field at old Kezar Stadium in San Francisco's Golden Gate Park. Kezar Stadium was rebuilt after the devastating 1989 earthquake.

One can only wonder if Cal's Memorial Stadium will suffer a similar fate anytime soon and that unpredictability makes it the most dangerous place to watch a game in the Bay Area.

WHERE'S THE BEST SEAT IN BAY AREA SPORTS?

12 The Bay Area's best free seat is on Tightwad Hill, perched amidst the woods above the northeast side of Cal's Memorial Stadium. Just bring a blanket, some beer, and perhaps some nose plugs if you don't want to inhale secondhand smoke. Hundreds of fans flock to that side of Strawberry Canyon on Saturdays to catch a glimpse of the Golden Bears, or, perhaps, the stunning panorama of the Bay Area. If you want in on the bargain, act now—the Tightwad Hill cheapskates might be losing their free view because of improvements planned for Memorial Stadium.

And keep in mind there are dangers with Tightwad Hill, as you might slide down the steep slope or blow out an eardrum if you're too close to Cal's Victory Cannon, which shoots off before each game and after each score.

Okay, so that's the best free seat. But say money's no object. Say you can sit anywhere you want for any Bay Area sporting event. Where do you plop your heinie in what truly can be called the best seat in the Bay Area's house?

We've got plenty of pro teams to choose from: The 49ers, Raiders, Giants, A's, Warriors, Sharks, and Earthquakes. And don't forget NASCAR's Sprint Cup race in Sonoma, where Turn 9 is the spot to be.

Decades ago, we didn't have such a multitude of options. But we did have Pacific Coast League baseball between the San Francisco Seals and Oakland Oaks. That cross-bay rivalry, which ended some 50 years ago, featured Sunday doubleheaders with one game at each team's home field. For some fans, this was paradise: Drinking your beer at the Oaks' park in Emeryville, then, ahem, leaving the beer at Seals Stadium in San Francisco.

Fast forward to this era if you will. An increasingly hot ticket is watching the fast-paced, free shooting Warriors. Oracle Arena was the-place-to-be during the Warriors' 2007 playoff run. Celebrities like Kate Hudson, Snoop Dogg, Jessica Alba, Woody Harrelson, Carlos Santana, and Penny Marshall came courtside to watch the Warriors battle the Dallas Mavericks and Utah Jazz. That excitement carried over to the following season, with 20,000 fans continually packing Oracle Arena and its chic clubs behind the stands. Courtside is the place to be, though. As hot a spot and as upclose to the action as those seats are, however, we can count on the Warriors making the play-offs, what, once every 13 thirteen years or so? Sorry, cheap shot. But, hey, at least they've become really fun to watch in recent seasons with Baron Davis running the floor in Don Nelson's up-tempo system.

On to baseball. Field-club seats behind home plate at AT&T Park provided an awesome sight (and the closest view) of Barry Bonds' pursuit of home-run records. Okay,

okay, a seat in a McCovey Cove kayak or a lucky spot in the bleachers might have been a better place to catch one of Bonds' valuable home-run balls. But those field-club seats were the equivalent of an NBA courtside spot, and plenty of dignitaries and celebrities preferred sitting there than in a kayak.

Good luck trying to convince anyone in the Bay Area that the best seat for a game is at the Giants' former home, down the shoreline off Candlestick Point. It's been nearly 50 years since Candlestick Park opened for business and began hosting the Giants, who actually began playing there in 1960. The 49ers moved into Candlestick in 1971, and they've been stuck there despite efforts to build a new stadium either on the same site, or nearby at the former Hunter's Point Naval Shipyard, or down in Santa Clara across the street from their training facility. Former 49ers owner Eddie DeBartolo Jr. once called Candlestick a "pigsty," and former St. Louis Cardinals manager Whitey Herzog called it "a toilet bowl with the lid up."

At the toilet bowl across the Bay, Oakland's McAfee Coliseum is like a fixer-upper house that just doesn't quite give you that at-home feel. It, too, is over 40 years old, opening in 1966 for the Raiders while the A's began taking shelter in 1968. Bring the binoculars if you're taking in an A's game, courtesy of the vast foul territory. Then again, the A's did do away with its highest seats, putting a tarp across its upper deck in 2006 to downsize capacity by about 10,000 seats, to 34,077. Good news came in 2008: Part of the upper deck was reopened as part of an all-you-can-eat buffet promotion. Or maybe that's bad news if unlimited hot dogs, nachos, peanuts, popcorn, soda, and ice cream don't fit into your diet. Although 64,000 can gather inside McAfee Coliseum for a Raiders game, only about 10,000 sideline seats offer premium viewing. But the most rowdy seats in the rowdiest of NFL houses remain in the south end zone's lower stands, home of The Black Hole. When Lane Kiffin was introduced as the Raiders coach in 2007, he told the media he asked that his family get season tickets in the Black Hole. Smart move, for you most certainly don't want a spot atop Mt. Davis, the 10,000-seat nosebleed section that was erected atop the stadium's East side in 1996.

This may come as a shock, but the best fan seat for a Bay Area sporting event is sitting inside San Jose's HP Pavilion for a San Jose Sharks playoff game. The Sharks have been nearly a perennial contender inside The Shark Tank.

It's not just that pro hockey is still somewhat of a novelty out here in the Bay Area. Anyone who's seen hockey in person will swear what a difference it is from watching the sport on television. Attending a Sharks playoff game brings that experience up a notch. You've got the chill from the ice, the fast-paced action by the teal-colored men on skates, the loud sounds that reverberate so well inside the Arena and, of course, you've got playoff hockey. You get all that pretty much wherever you sit inside the Pavilion. But for the best seat in that house—and the best one, period, in the Bay Area—don't be so sure it's in the touted corners (great viewing angle) or up against the glass (close to the action). No, if you want the best, you better snag one about 10 rows up from center ice. There, your views aren't impaired by the glass, you're still close to the action and you can hear the hits, shots, and chatter as well. So drop your heinie there when it's time to drop the puck in the playoffs.

WHAT'S THE BEST CALL BY A BAY AREA BROADCASTER?

 13

This one's a no-brainer.

Surely you've seen replays of The Play that Cal's 1982 football team used to stun Stanford (and the nation). If so, you've also likely heard The Call made by Cal's radio voice, Joe Starkey. Many Cal fans have Starkey's verses memorized, and one booster even has a website named after Starkey's most dramatic description of The Play: "The band is out on the field!"

Euphoria reigned, not just on the play and on the field, but on the airwaves. Okay, so Starkey never used the word "lateral" in his initial play-by-play description of the five-lateral kickoff return for a touchdown, and he didn't identify the participants by name, other than two references to "Rodgers." But that's what helped make the call so epic, that Starkey got caught up in the bizarre finish and showed unparalleled enthusiasm.

Here's The Call: "All right, here we go with the kickoff. Harmon will probably try to squib it and he does. The ball comes loose and the Bears have to get out of bounds. Rodgers is along the sideline, another one (lateral)....They're still in deep trouble at midfield, they tried to do a couple of (laterals) ...The ball is still loose as they get it to Rodgers! They get it back now to the 30, they're down to the 20 ...Oh, the band is out on the field!! He's gonna go into the end zone! He's gone into the end zone!!"

Once officials conferred and ruled it a valid touchdown, Starkey erupted again: "THE BEARS HAVE WON! THE BEARS HAVE WON! Oh my God! The most amazing, sensational, dramatic, heart-rending... exciting, thrilling finish in the history of college football!"

Starkey didn't stop there, though. He's continued on as Cal's radio voice, as well as the 49ers,' whom he provided a memorable call by shouting "Owens! Owens! Owens!" on Terrell Owens' game-winning touchdown catch in the 1998 49ers' wild-card playoff game against the Green Bay Packers.

Owens' play is known as The Catch II in 49ers' lore. But what are the contenders for The Call II in Bay Area sports broadcasting history?

Let's give the nod to Bill King's description of The Holy Roller, a last-second play that lifted the Raiders past the host San Diego Chargers on Sept. 10, 1978. We could describe The Holy Roller as a play in which Raiders quarterback Ken Stabler fumbled the ball forward, and it was eventually scooped up in the end zone by Dave Casper for a game-winning touchdown.

Of Course, King described it much better: "The ball, flipped forward, is loose. A wild scramble. Two seconds on the clock. Casper grabbing the ball. It is ruled a fumble.

49

Casper has recovered in the end zone. The Oakland Raiders have scored on the most zany, unbelievable, absolutely impossible dream of a play. Madden is on the field. He wants to know if it's real. They said yes, get your big butt out of here. He does. There's nothing real in the world anymore. The Raiders have won the football game."

Two seasons earlier, King was capping off his call of the Raiders' victory in Super Bowl XI when Willie Brown returned an interception for a touchdown: "Old man Willie! He's going all the way!"

Okay, not all great calls were about touchdowns—no offense to Greg Papa's signature line: "Touchdown, Raiders!"

In 1964, Minnesota Vikings defensive end Jim Marshall thought he returned a 49ers fumble for a touchdown. As Lon Simmons called it: "Marshall is running the wrong way! And he's running it into the end zone the wrong way, thinks he has scored a touchdown. He has scored a safety!"

Simmons's catchphrase during his decades-long stints covering the Giants and A's has been: "Tell it goodbye!" King had a familiar line, too: "Holy Toledo!" Russ Hodges signature home-run call for the Giants: "Tell it, 'Bye-bye baby.' "

Jack "The Old Walnut Farmer" Macdonald thrilled San Francisco Seals fans decades ago by announcing home runs that were going, going, gone, "right through Aunt Maggie's window!" But what about all those calls of Barry Bonds' record-setting homers? Of course, we can't leave those out of here.

* When Bonds broke Mark McGwire's single-season record with his 71st home run on October 5, 2001, Jon Miller called it as: "There's a high drive deep into right centre field, to the big part of the ballpark ... NUMBER 71! And what a shot over the 421 foot marker!"

* When Bonds passed Hank Aaron for the all-time home run mark on August. 7, 2007, Miller described number 756 as: "Everybody standing here at 24 Willie Mays Plaza. An armada of nautical craft gathered in McCovey Cove beyond the right-field wall. Bonds one home run away from history, and he swings and there's a long one. Deep into right-center field. Way back there. It's gone! A home run! ... Into the center-field bleachers to the left of the 421-foot marker. An extraordinary shot to the deepest part of the yard ... And Barry Bonds with 756 home runs. He has hit more home runs than anyone who has ever played the game."

* FOX Sports Net's Duane Kuiper's call of 756 on the TV side: "And Bonds hits one hard. Hits it DEEP! It is outta here! 756! Bonds stands alone! He is on top of the all-time home-run list. What a special moment for Barry Bonds. And what a special moment for these fans here in San Francisco."

* Kuiper had a similar TV call on Bonds' 715th homer that passed Babe Ruth: "Bonds hits one high, hits it deep to center. Outta here! 715!"—and that call is the only full one the Giants can archive. Over in the Giants' radio booth,

51

Dave Flemming's microphone cut out after he said: "Three-and-two. Finley runs. The payoff pitch, a swing and a drive to deep cen ...."

The most famous call in Giants franchise history is undoubtedly Hodges's call of Bobby Thompson's home run that lifted the New York Giants past the Brooklyn Dodgers in the 1951 regular-season finale. That soundtrack—"The Giants win the pennant! The Giants win the pennant!"—was pulled out of the archives in April 2008, but not for baseball purposes. KNBR's Gary Radnich, the reigning king of Bay Area sports broadcasting, compared Hodges's euphoric call to the one that San Jose Sharks' broadcaster Randy Hahn let rip after Joe Thornton's game-winning goal in a first-round playoff win at Calgary. "HE SCORES! HE SCORES! HE SCORES!" Hahn proclaimed after Douglas Murray's slapshot got tipped into the net by Thornton in the final seconds of a Game 4 victory.

A debate about memorable calls isn't complete without mentioning Stanford's Bob Murphy. He served 43 years as the voice of Stanford's football and basketball teams. A 1988 upset by Stanford's basketball team provided the top moment from Murphy's microphone. The Cardinal was in the Elite Eight in St. Louis when a dunk by forward Mark Madsen sealed a 79–77 win over Rhode Island. Murphy's call: "Madsen stuffed it! ... AND! ... HE! ... WAS! ... FOULED!"

Murphy's final game as The Voice of The Cardinal was the 2007 Big Game, and as he wisely noted during the final minutes of host Stanford's upset over Cal, there was no sight of any band members on the field this time. Starkey couldn't have said it any better in the booth next door, though he surely would have said it with less enthusiasm than his ultimate call of The Play 25 years earlier.

WHO'S THE BAY AREA'S MOST BELOVED OWNER OF ALL TIME?

 Love 'em or hate 'em, that's how it goes when describing Bay Area fans' feelings for the owners of their beloved (or hated) pro franchises.

Let's look at the San Francisco Giants' ownership. Some will hail Horace Stoneham for moving the club West from New York in 1958 and thus bringing major league baseball to the region. Others might celebrate Bob Lurie's group for buying the Giants from Stoneham in 1976 and staving off a potential move to Toronto. The Giants again were on the threshold of relocating—this time to Tampa—when Lurie agreed to sell in December 1992 to a group of local investors, headed by then-Safeway CEO Peter Magowan.

Magowan's group not only kept the Giants in San Francisco, they provided the club a new, picturesque home. In 2000, the Giants moved into that ballpark—now called AT&T Park—on the waterfront near downtown. They also brought in Barry Bonds in 1993, and a leading proponent in keeping Bonds through 2007 was the Burns family, which owns the biggest stake in the club. Sue Burns, who took over that share in the Giants following the 2006 death of her husband Harmon, led the cheers for Bonds during his 2007 grasp of the all-time home run record.

When it comes to franchise relocations, the Raiders take the cake, and that's one mighty reason why Al Davis' stature among the Raider Nation has wavered. The Raiders' round-trip voyage went from Oakland to Los Angeles (in 1982) and back to Oakland (in 1995). The Raiders won Super Bowls representing both cities, and through it all, Davis has served as their unmistakable icon. But he's also been condemned by even the most ardent Raider fans during the swoon that followed the 2002 team's 48–21 blowout loss in Super Bowl XXXVII against Tampa Bay.

The Bay Area's been home to a more eccentric and outrageous owner than Davis. Charlie Finley's wild tenure as the A's owner included, of course, moving the franchise from Kansas City to Oakland in 1968. Finley soon saw his club win three straight World Series crowns from 1972–74, and one rallying cry was the players' hatred of Finley. He had gimmicks—mustache bounties for players, orange baseballs, a mechanical rabbit delivering balls to umpires—but he certainly didn't have widespread love in the Bay Area. The Haas family, which bought the A's from Finley, drew great admiration. Current A's owner Lew Wolff has the potential to gain huge popularity points if his plan for a new stadium in Fremont comes to fruition in 2012, but only if the A's fan base accepts such a move out of Oakland.

The A's next-door neighbors, the Golden State Warriors, have seen their principal owner endure more boos than cheers. Fans unmercifully booed Chris Cohan during the 2000 NBA All-Star Game in Oakland, but seven years later, they were high-fiving him in his courtside seat during the Warriors' magical playoff run.

The most famous owner in Warriors history, however, is the one who moved the franchise from Philadelphia to the Bay Area and owned the club for 23 years. That man is Franklin Mieuli, who not only owns a ring from the Warriors' 1975 championship season, but also five Super Bowl rings by way of his minority ownership in the 49ers. Mieuli, also a former minority owner of the Giants, remains a fixture at Warriors games and wears his familiar Sherlock Holmes cap in his courtside seat.

But the most revered, most famous, and most successful owner in Bay Area sports history is none other than Eddie DeBartolo Jr., whose 49ers won five Super Bowls during his reign.

He lavished his players with money and affection, and more importantly, he delivered the Bay Area a championship-winning franchise that dominated the NFL for much of his 21 years as the 49ers' owner.

The 49er faithful's love for him remains strong to this day, even after a Louisiana gaming scandal pushed him out of the NFL in the late 1990s. He sold his interests in the franchise in 1998 to his sister, Denise DeBartolo York, who turned over day-to-day control of the 49ers to her husband, John York, a NFL neophyte who's had a dismal reign both in terms of the team's win-loss record and a stalled quest to build a new stadium.

The Yorks' failures have kept alive the Bay Area's infatuation with Eddie D. When some 8,000 fans turned out for Bill Walsh's memorial service at Monster Park in July 2007, they chanted "Ed-die! Ed-die!" every 15 minutes. A similar sound reverberated through that stadium in 2003, when DeBartolo attended a 49ers game in which Hall of Fame defensive back Ronnie Lott's jersey was retired at halftime.

"Playing for Eddie was a pleasure. We bet the farm," former 49ers quarterback Steve Young said in his 2005 Pro Football Hall of Fame induction speech. "How could you not love playing for Eddie? The rumors were true. He was the best."

DeBartolo was inducted into the Bay Area Sports Hall of Fame in April 2008, and consider him enshrined here as the Bay Area's most beloved owner.

WHO'S THE BIGGEST VILLAIN TO BAY AREA SPORTS FANS?

 The initial inclination is to name Tommy Lasorda, Charles Barkley, or one of several Dallas Cowboys as the top villain in the Bay Area sports scene. But maybe our most despised sports figures aren't even out-of-towners. Let's investigate.

One simple sentence in the 1984 classic movie Fletch sums up how San Francisco Giants fans feel about their number one archenemy. In that endearing scene, Fletch, played by Chevy Chase, is in the Los Angeles police chief's office and points to a picture of the chief and Lasorda. "I hate Tommy Lasorda," says Fletch, who then throws a right hook into the picture and breaks its glass.

Bay Area fans love to chant "Beat L.A.," and Lasorda has played out as the perfect villain for that anti-L.A. sentiment. Ever the showman, Lasorda played to the Candlestick Park crowd, blowing kisses and tipping his cap to fans while they fervently booed him. Videos of Giants fans booing him even can be found on YouTube, nearly 20 years after those boo fests.

Giants' fans have others to loathe, too. Former New York Yankees second baseman Bobby Richardson sealed his fate in Giants lore when he caught Willie McCovey's line drive to end the 1962 World Series, stranding Willie Mays and Matty Alou on base in the Giants' 1–0 loss.

You might think another contender for top villain is former Giants slugger Barry Bonds. But the Bay Area hasn't hated Bonds anywhere close to how he's perceived across the nation. Bonds, actually, has been much more embraced and celebrated than vilified by Bay Area fans, so strike him from our discussions here.

Over the years, Giants fans have been willing to turn on their own. Shortstop Johnnie LeMaster was so unpopular that in one 1979 game he wore the word "BOO" in place of his name on the back of his jersey. He should have saved that jersey for Giants closer Armando Benitez, whose two and a half seasons with the club were marked by blown saves, a bad hamstring, and a poor demeanor. When the Giants traded Benitez two months into the 2007 season, General Manager Brian Sabean sounded almost reluctant in making the move, noting that it was fans, the media, and some players who "felt he needed to go."

A couple months earlier, the Bay Area had found itself the next Lasorda, another wannabe villain in Charles Barkley, a former NBA star turned TNT broadcaster. Barkley so despised the Warriors' 2007 playoff run that he repeatedly called it "a national nightmare." But Barkley's teasing didn't stop there. He went on to degrade the Bay Area's surroundings, saying he'd prefer staying on Alcatraz than in San Francisco or Oakland. Barkley also served as a reminder of the Warriors' 12-year playoff drought. Prior to their 2007 playoff run, the Warriors last made the postseason in 1994, when they were swept by the Phoenix Suns and gave up 56 points to Barkley in that series' finale.

If the 49ers didn't have five Lombardi Trophies in the lobby at team headquarters, there'd probably be more grudges held about opponents who doomed them. That list could include Roger Staubach, for his 1972 comeback win over the 49ers in the playoffs; or any of The Triplets during their mid-1990s dominance, including running back Emmitt Smith, boisterous wide receiver Michael Irvin and quarterback Troy Aikman, who ignited the first of his three Super Bowl runs when he found Alvin Harper on a 70-yard play that helped clinch the Cowboys' win over the 49ers in the 1992 NFC Championship Game.

Those Cowboys legends are more respected by Bay Area fans than truly reviled. Now, as for the cross-bay Raiders, here's a name that will live in infamy: Walt Coleman, the referee who enforced the formerly unheard of "Tuck Rule" in the 2001 Raiders' loss to eventual Super Bowl champion New England.

All that said, the Bay Area's top villain is a role shared in recent years not by an opponent, but actually the embattled leaders of the 49ers and Raiders. If 49ers owners John York and Denise DeBartolo York aren't being vilified by the media and fans for their franchise's failures, another likely target is whomever they've got coaching their team, from Steve Mariucci (fired after 2002), to Dennis Erickson (fired after 2004), to Mike Nolan (nearly fired after 2007).

The same holds true across the Bay. Even though Raiders managing general partner Al Davis has much more clout and football knowledge than the 49ers' stewards, he, too, has drawn the wrath of Raiders faithful. Not only did he turn off Oakland's fan base by moving the franchise to Los Angeles from 1982–94, but Davis has overseen the club's collapse since a 2002 run to the Super Bowl. The Raiders' typical scapegoat hasn't been Davis as much as it's been his coaches, from Bill Callahan (fired after 2003), to Norv Turner (fired after 2005), to Art Shell (fired after 2006), to Lane Kiffin (nearly a goner after 2007).

We may not realize it, but, it's true that we reserve most of our contempt for the leaders of our NFL franchises. Pro football rules the Bay Area, and when the 49ers and Raiders are not doing well, their owners and coaches take more heat from fans and media than Tommy Lasorda, Charles Barkley, or any Dallas Cowboy ever endured.

WHAT WAS THE WORST RELATIONSHIP BETWEEN A PLAYER AND COACH?

16 When 49ers quarterback Alex Smith and Coach Mike Nolan sniped at each other in the media about Smith's bum shoulder in 2007, it made for a decent controversy. But, compared to other player-vs.-coach scandals, Smith-Nolan barely registers a blip on the Sprewell Scale. Yes, that's the standard that's been set for all player-vs.-coach feuds, stemming from Latrell Sprewell's 1997 choking of Warriors coach P.J. Carlesimo.

It's December 1, 1997, the Warriors are practicing, and first-year Coach Carlesimo tells Sprewell to work harder. Sprewell responds by reportedly choking Carlesimo, forcing him to the floor, and leaving scrapes on the coach's neck. Sprewell left the gym, only to return 15 minutes later and resume the altercation.

Initially banished from the NBA, Sprewell ended up only sitting out the Warriors' remaining 68 games of that 1997–98 season, a 19–63 campaign. Sprewell was then traded to the New York Knicks, and he helped lead them (an eighth seed) into the NBA Finals. Carlesimo, meanwhile, got fired on December 27, 1999, leaving with a

46–113 overall record (.289 winning percentage) that included the Warriors' 6–21 start that season.

Can anything measure up to this gem?

Well, Sprewell-Carlesimo wasn't the first Warriors player-coach dispute to draw headlines. Ten years after a feud between center Joe Barry Carroll and Coach John Bach, much more drama ensued between Chris Webber and Don Nelson. After winning Rookie of the Year honors in 1994, Webber couldn't take Nelson as his coach anymore and, the following season, he forced a trade that haunted the Warriors for the next decade. No choking there, just some hurt feelings on Webber's part for the way Nelson allegedly treated and talked about him.

Some called it a power struggle, some termed it an ego battle, and some accurately predicted it was the end of a playoff-contending franchise. A 50-win playoff team in 1993–94, the Warriors traded Webber to the Washington Bullets in November 1994 for Tom Gugliatta and three first-round draft picks. So began a Warriors freefall that saw Nelson resign in February 1995 and the team finish 26–56. The Warriors fell out of playoff contention ... for the next 12 years!

But then, in February 2008, Webber was back with the Warriors, reuniting with Nellie and making nice before Webber retired less than two months later. It's hard to win this argument with that kind of fight.

Let's try football. Four years after they contended for the Super Bowl, the 2006 Raiders had quite a sideshow to accompany their 2–14 campaign. That player-vs.-coach drama started shortly upon Art Shell's arrival as the Raiders coach in February. His get-to-know-you meeting with wide receiver Jerry Porter turned into a get-out-of-my-office and get-into-the-doghouse situation.

Porter demanded a trade, lost his starting job, was suspended four games for conduct detrimental to the team—the league reduced it to a two-game suspension—and he caught one pass in the four games he sparingly played. Porter returned the following season, but Shell didn't, as the 2–14 effort cost him his job. It also put an end to a short-lived feud that did nothing more than serve as a small sideshow to that season's trainwreck.

Another contender is a feud that ensued with the Bay Area's other NFL franchise. The best verbal volleys between moody wide receiver Terrell Owens and happy-go-lucky coach Steve Mariucci came midway through the 2001 season. That's when Owens claimed Mariucci's "buddy system" with other coaches around the league prevented the 49ers from running up the score or finishing off opponents. Owens' verbal blast came three days after the 49ers blew a 19-point lead and lost a 37–31 overtime game at Chicago. Mariucci called Owens' accusation "the most utterly ridiculous statement I've ever read and completely void of any deep thought." And, to think, four years earlier, Owens was crying on Mariucci's shoulder after making a game-winning touchdown catch in a wild-card playoff game against Green Bay.

Now if you wanted to expand the debate of best Bay Area sports feuds, we've got some contenders that weren't player-vs.-coach.

There's been owner-vs.-player, such as the majority of the Oakland A's roster rallying against owner Charlie Finley during their World Series hat trick from 1972–74.

There's been owner-vs.-league (see: the Raiders' Al Davis vs. the NFL).

There's been owner-vs.-coach (see: Davis vs. Mike Shanahan).

There's been owner-vs.-city officials (see: Davis vs. Oakland, and the 49ers' John York vs. San Francisco Mayor Gavin Newsom).

And, of course, there've been player-vs.-player (see: Barry Bonds vs. Jeff Kent in the Giants dugout in 2002, or any number of clubhouse fracases during the 1970s A's dynasty).

But, alas, nothing quite lives up to the Sprewell Scale, and that attack on Carlesimo is one that has stood as the standard bearer for a decade, and perhaps many decades to come.

65

WHAT'S THE BEST BAY AREA SPORTS MOVIE?

 17

If not for DVDs and videotapes of past championship runs by Bay Area teams, you could barely say any sports movie was filmed here.

San Francisco has served as a majestic backdrop for so many movies and television shows, to be sure, but car chases down the hilly streets don't count for "Best Athletic Performance."

Instead, we have *The Fan*, Wesley Snipes and Robert DeNiro's dramatic tale of a knife-selling stalker who goes overboard in his support of Barry Bonds, er, Bobby Rayburn, an All-Star ballplayer who comes off as arrogant as Bonds.

It's a decent thriller. But, gosh, is that 1996 flick all we can offer the Academy? Ah yes, there are a couple more options.

But Samuel L. Jackson's role in *Coach Carter* didn't exactly stir memories of his Oscar-nominated *Pulp Fiction* days, did it? *Coach Carter* was based on Richmond High School's 1999 boys basketball lockout, in which the coach (Ken Carter) didn't let his players resume their 13–0 start to the season unless they raised their grades. Even at the time, it seemed like a perfect Hollywood tale. Some of his rival coaches, however, cheapened Carter's intentions by calling it all a publicity stunt. Nevertheless, *Coach Carter* is still an inspiring tale.

The movie *Angels* in the Outfield has a Bay Area link even though it's based off the California Angels, down the road in Anaheim. That "Angels" outfield actually belonged to the Oakland A's, or, specifically, the Oakland-Alameda County Coliseum, as it was known during the movie's 1994 release.

Across the bay at Candlestick, several commercials have been filmed, as were scenes from some old-time movies—the 1962 thriller *Experiment in Terror* and the 1973 comedy *Freebie and the Bean*.

There is another "Bay Area sports movie" on the horizon. HBO bought the rights to the book *Game of Shadows*, which chronicled the steroid scandal involving Barry Bonds and the BALCO affair.

It's surprising, though, that there haven't been more sports-oriented movies set in the Bay Area. San Francisco offers a picturesque skyline, and the Bay Area's been home to many a sports scandal, not to mention several storybook championship runs. (And, no, we can't really count *Sports Illustrated's* compilation video of the 49ers' glory years, Pure Gold.)

Some of the most athletic feats in recent movies were produced by an East Bay studio, that being animation giant Pixar, which is based in Emeryville. So if you count Buzz Lightyear's and Woody's death defying feats in *Toy Story*, or the swift auto racing in *Cars*, then maybe those were the Bay's best sports movies. Or perhaps it was one of the handful of surfing documentaries filmed at the big-wave mecca known as Mavericks near Half Moon Bay.

Let's stray a little further from the norm and consider that the Bay Area's best sports video footage might come not in the form of a movie, but video games. The Bay Area is home to EA Sports' headquarters, that being in Redwood Shores. EA was launched in 1982, and it churns out the most popular sports video games on the planet, including the "Madden" football series as well as those for NBA basketball and FIFA soccer.

Sure, all these options may seem like a stretch, but that's what you have to resort to when The Fan is your region's leading sports movie. Damn, to think George Lucas calls the Bay Area home. Couldn't he have used the Golden Gate Bridge as the setting for a *Star Wars* spinoff related to sports?

WHO IS THE BAY AREA'S MOST PRESTIGIOUS FATHER-SON COMBO?

 Like father, like son, huh? In several cases, yes, a son has followed his father onto the Bay Area sports stage. Perhaps someday, with the continued growth of women's athletics, there'll be a handful of mother-daughter combos that also rivet the Bay Area sportspages (or Web pages.) But, for now, which father-son legacy has carved the biggest niche in our sports scene? Let's break down five possibilities:

5. THE NOLANS

Mike Nolan couldn't do what his dad Dick did for the 49ers, which was to coach them into the playoffs by his third season on the job. Dick Nolan's third year, 1970, actually produced the 49ers' first NFL playoff berth, using it to surprise Minnesota before falling in the NFC Championship Game to Dallas. Dick Nolan's teams in 1971 and '72 were ousted in the playoffs by the Cowboys, and while his 54–53–5 record through eight seasons is just above .500, it's a heck of a lot better than the 16–32 mark his son Mike produced from 2005–07. Following in your father's footsteps to an NFL head coaching gig is a rarity, however, as that feat was also pulled off only by the Shula, Mora, and Phillips families. Before passing away in 2007 after battling Alzheimer's and prostate cancer, Dick Nolan got to see his son rise through the ranks and assume the 49ers' post, making them the first father-son act to coach the same team since Wade Phillips succeeded his father with the New Orleans Saints during the 1985 season.

4. THE ALOUS

Although Felipe Alou represented the Giants in the 1962 All-Star Game and was famously joined by his brothers Matty and Jesus in the Giants outfield in 1963, he didn't deliver an extraordinary impact as the Giants manager, especially when his son, Moises, played for him in the 2005 and '06 season. Although Felipe guided the Giants to the National League West title in his first year as their manager in 2003, and Moises made the 2005 All-Star team, neither Alou returned to their roles in 2007. It seemed like a heart-warming move to bring father and son together, but Giants fans wanted more success out of them, not back-to-back third-place finishes (and sub-.500 records) in 2005 and '06.

3. THE BARRYS

Mention the name "Barry," and you might think of Bonds. But we'll get to him later. The Barry surname is synonymous with Bay Area basketball. Hall of Famer Rick Barry captained the Warriors to a dramatic sweep of the

Washington Bullets in the 1975 NBA Finals. He's known for so much more, too, whether it be other on-court achievements, or his legendary underhanded free throws, or his outspoken nature that has led him to another career in broadcasting, including a sports-talk gig with KNBR radio from 2001–06.

Barry has four sons that played basketball at Concord's De La Salle High School before following dad into the NBA: Jon (a 47 percent three-point shooter in 1995–96 with the Warriors), Drew (eight games with the Warriors in 1999–2000), Scooter, and Brent, who won NBA championships with the San Antonio Spurs in 2005 and '07. Rick and Brent are only the second father-son combo to each have won an NBA title.

2. THE ELWAYS

The name Elway dominated Bay Area college sports for a solid decade. While John Elway was starring at Stanford, his dad, Jack, was pioneering the spread offense down the road as San Jose State's coach from 1979–83. John finished his Stanford career in 1982 as the NCAA Division I leader in pass attempts, completions, and 200-yard games. He was a senior All-American, the Heisman Trophy runner-up, and, oh yeah, a top baseball prospect. Stanford wasn't without an Elway for long after John left The Farm. Jack coached the Cardinal from 1984–88. Unlike his son, Jack took the Cardinal to a bowl game, albeit a 1986 loss in the

Gator Bowl. John was denied a shot at a bowl game thanks to the final play of his final season, The Play which lifted Cal past Stanford in 1982's Big Game.

1. THE BONDSES

Of the 100-plus father-son duos that reached baseball's big leagues, none combined for more home runs than Bobby and Barry Bonds. No father-son combo in Bay Area sports history can match the stamp they put on the region, either.

The Bondses are the only players in major league history to both hit 30-plus home runs and steal 30-plus bases in the same season five times. Their statistics are phenomenal, of course, and their contribution to the Giants is just as mighty.

But, first, examine some of the Bonds' stats. Bobby played the first seven seasons of his 14-year career in San Francisco, where he collected all three of his Gold Gloves and two of his three All-Star Game selections. After seven years in Pittsburgh, Barry played the next 15 in San Francisco, hitting 586 home runs there en route to the all-time home-run record, which stood at 762 after the 2007 season. All but two of Barry's 14 All-Star game selections came as a Giant, where he also won five of eight Gold Gloves and five of his seven National League MVP awards.

One special link in the Bonds' legacy is how much Barry relied on his father's hitting advice. Once Barry arrived in San Francisco in 1993, Bobby spent the first four years as the Giants' hitting coach before moving into the personnel department (but continuing to critique his son's hitting approach.) And while Barry Bonds received a ton of criticism from media and fans in his final seasons with the Giants, there's no disputing this father-son duo's impact on Bay Area sports.

49ERS

WHICH 49ERS' SUPER BOWL TEAM WAS THE BEST?

19 When the 1989 49ers claimed the franchise's fourth Super Bowl, Los Angeles Rams Coach John Robinson wrote a piece for The Associated Press trumpeting that 49ers team as the best he'd ever seen in his days in the NFL. True or False?

To be fair, we also need to look at the 1981 breakthrough champs, the 1984 one-loss squad, the 1988 team that won the Super Bowl in thrilling fashion to send Bill Walsh out in style, and the 1994 free-agent-filled unit.

The 1981 team always will have a special place in 49ers' fans hearts, because, as they say, you never forget your first … Super Bowl winner. We celebrated "The Catch" by Dwight Clark, and, two weeks later, an epic goal-line stand in the Pontiac Silverdome during the franchise's first Super Bowl victory. Joe Montana won the first of his three Super Bowl MVP awards, and the dynasty was underway.

The 49ers' best Super Bowl finish undoubtedly came from the 1988 team. After an inconsistent 10–6 regular season, the 49ers left no doubt in the postseason that their third Lombardi Trophy would be coming home from Miami. The playoffs began with Montana connecting with

Rice for three touchdowns in a 34–9 rout of the Minnesota Vikings, who eliminated the 49ers a year earlier in a divisional playoff game. The 49ers then defied the chilly elements awaiting them in Soldier Field, posting a 28–3 win in the NFC Championship Game, the 49ers delivering the stifling defense while Montana connected with Rice for two first-half touchdowns to help set the tone. They won Super Bowl XXIII by beating Cincinnati 20–16 on Montana's touchdown pass to John Taylor with 34 seconds remaining. That sent Walsh out a winner in his 10th and final season as coach. That team also had so many key characters in the 49ers dynasty: Montana, Walsh, Jerry Rice, Ronnie Lott, Keena Turner, Michael Carter, Charles Haley, and Roger Craig, who led the 49ers in both rushing (1,502 yards) and receptions (76, for 534 yards).

The 49ers' fifth—and last, at this rate—Super Bowl season in 1994 was tremendous, too. Steve Young finally broke out of Montana's shadow and notched his first Super Bowl win as the 49ers' starting QB, throwing a record six touchdown passes in the 49–26 rout of San Diego for the Lombardi trophy. That squad overflowed with talent, thanks in large part to the advent of free agency. It took a while to mesh that influx of free agents— Deion Sanders, Ken Norton Jr., Gary Plummer, Richard Dent, Rickey Jackson, among others—and the 1994 49ers started off 3–2.

The 1989 49ers can make a strong case they were the franchise's best when you encapsulate regular-season dominance with postseason domination. Montana's final Super Bowl triumph came with that 1989 team, and what a run it was to cap off the 49ers' "Team of the Decade" dominance. Montana posted a career best 112.4 passer rating and won league MVP honors as the 49ers ripped through a 14–2 regular season. George Seifert, in his first season as coach, kept alive the momentum Walsh created, with the obvious help of great players such as Montana, Rice, Lott, Craig, and Haley.

The 1989 49ers absolutely obliterated their postseason foes: 41–13 vs. Minnesota, 30–3 vs. the Los Angeles Rams and, the crème de la crème, 55–10 vs. Denver in a Big Easy Super Bowl. No one will confuse the Rams and Broncos with enormous hurdles to clear, however, so we'll have to keep the 1989 team off the pedestal reserved for Greatest 49er Team Ever.

And that throne belongs to the 1984 team, which went 18–1, an amazing record that only the 1985 Chicago Bears (Super Bowl champs) and 2007 New England Patriots (Super Bowl runners up) have equaled.

Yes, the 1984 team predated Rice's era by a year, but Montana still thrived with an offensive cast including Craig, Dwight Clark, Freddie Soloman, Russ Francis, Wendell Tyler, Randy Cross, and Keith Fahnhorst. These 49ers produced the first 15–1 season in NFL history , and it was capped by a 38–16 Super Bowl win over the Miami Dolphins and hotshot quarterback Dan Marino, who had set a single-season record with 48 touchdown passes, and 5,084 passing yards that year.

Not many folks thought the 49ers could deny Marino a victory in what turned out to be his only Super Bowl appearance. But the 49ers defense answered that challenge, as it had so many others throughout the season. None of their final eight regular-season opponents scored more than 17 points, and the Bay Area embraced defensive maestros such as Lott, Turner, Dwaine Board, Fred Dean, Michael Carter, Riki Ellison, Hacksaw Reynolds, Dwight Hicks, Eric Wright, and Carlton Williamson.

The 49ers' only loss all season: A 20–17 at home in October against the Pittsburgh Steelers. Were they humbled? Motivated? Probably both, and they wouldn't lose again. Nor would they have to play outside of the Bay Area after December 2. Their final two regular-season games were at Candlestick Park, as were their first two playoff dalliances before the Super Bowl triumph at Stanford Stadium. The playoff run began with a 21–10 divisional-round win over the New York Giants, then the 49ers defense registered nine sacks in a 23–0 shutout of Walter Payton's Chicago Bears.

Craig and Tyler, a year after both joined the 49ers, combined to rush for 1,911 yards in 1984, and although Tyler accounted for 1,262 of those yards, Craig also chipped in with a team-leading 71 receptions for 675 yards. Montana's other popular targets included Dwight Clark, Earl Cooper, and Freddie Solomon, who had a team-high 10 touchdown catches.

The best team in 49ers history capped off the franchise's best season with that surprising rout of the Dolphins in the Super Bowl. Craig scored three touchdowns, Wright and Lott each had an interception, Board had a couple key sacks, and Montana worked his magic (331 yards, three touchdown passes) to outduel a fellow Western Pennsylvania product, Marino, who went down firing 50 passes. And so a third Lombardi Trophy headed for the case while this 49ers team took its place atop all others in the franchise's illustrious lore.

WHAT WERE JOE MONTANA'S TOP FIVE GAMES (EXCLUDING SUPER BOWLS)?

20 In his first season as the 49ers' full-time starting quarterback, Joe Montana quickly found out what it was like to win a Super Bowl, doing so in Detroit. Three years later, he won another, outdueling Miami Dolphins' gunslinger Dan Marino at Stanford Stadium. In 1988, Montana led the 49ers on a magical comeback drive to secure their third Super Bowl, topping the Cincinnati Bengals in Tampa. A year later, he set a Super Bowl record with five touchdown passes in a rout of the Denver Broncos in New Orleans.

His legacy is forever solidified behind those Super Bowl triumphs, not to mention his 122 passes without an interception in those games. But Montana had so many other classic moments in his Hall of Fame career, and here are the top five:

5. DECEMBER 28, 1992: 49ERS 24, LIONS 6

Elbow woes sidelined him all of 1991 and all but this final game of 1992. His final curtain call unfolded after halftime, when he completed 15 of 21 passes for 126 yards and two touchdowns for the NFC West-champion 49ers. His arms shot up in the air in trademark fashion after a touchdown toss to Brent Jones, and a rain-soaked crowd of nearly 56,000 chanted "Joe! Joe! Joe!" after a scoring strike to Amp Lee in the closing minutes. Yep, Montana still had the magic. But this was Steve Young's team by now. Young had wrapped up a second straight NFL passing title, would be named league MVP and, in a few months, would prevail in the Joe vs. Steve debate once Montana got traded to Kansas City. Don't say this game was meaningless for the 49ers simply because they had already secured home-field advantage in the NFC playoffs, an advantage that didn't pan out in an NFC Championship Game loss to Dallas. This game had plenty of meaning, as the 49er Faithful got to see Montana in vintage form one last time at the end of a game.

4. SEPTEMBER 11, 1988: 49ERS 20, GIANTS 17

Montana replaced Young in the second half of a tied game and rallied the 49ers to victory, shaking off a troubled elbow and throwing a 78-yard touchdown pass to Jerry Rice on third down in the final minute at the Meadowlands. That Montana-to-Rice connection—ah, a beautiful phrase if there ever was one—served as the perfect countermeasure to Phil Simms's touchdown pass only 39 seconds earlier that gave the Giants a 17–13 lead. Montana and Rice hooked up for 55 touchdowns in their career, which is surprisingly 30 fewer times than Young and Rice connected.

3. DECEMBER 7, 1980: 49ERS 38, SAINTS 35 (OT)

Of Montana's 31 career fourth-quarter comeback wins, his first went down as the greatest regular-season comeback in NFL history. The 49ers overcame a 35–7 halftime deficit, Montana and Clark began their fantastic rapport, and Bill Walsh had himself a new starting quarterback. The Saints, meanwhile, fell to 0–14 when Ray Wersching's 36-yard field goal won it for the 49ers in overtime. The opposing quarterback that day was Archie Manning, who had the Saints out to a 21–0 lead before the 49ers even got a first down. Freddie Solomon's 57-yard punt return produced the 49ers only first-half points. Then Montana went to work, producing four scoring drives that each went at least 78 yards. Montana even ran for a touchdown. So long Steve DeBerg, hello Joe Cool.

2. SEPTEMBER 24, 1989: 49ERS 38, EAGLES 28

Sacked eight times through the first three quarters and trailing 21–10, Montana answered Buddy Ryan's famed "46 defense" by tossing four touchdowns in the fourth quarter. Yes, the 49ers were serious about defending their Super Bowl title, and these cocky Eagles would get humbled on their home field. Neither defensive end Reggie White nor hotshot Eagles quarterback Randall Cunningham could steal the show from Montana. He completed 11 of his final 12 passes for 227 yards, and overall he went 25–for–34 for 428 yards. Rather than sit on a 31–28 lead, Montana converted a Ronnie Lott interception into a fifth touchdown pass, finding Jerry Rice for a 33-yarder on third-and-four with two minutes remaining. The Team of The 80's was alive and well.

1. JANUARY 10, 1982: 49ERS 28, COWBOYS 27

The turning point in the 49ers franchise came in this NFC Championship Game thriller over the Cowboys. The game is known for "The Catch" that Dwight Clark made in the final minute for the winning touchdown. But don't forget Montana's throw, which he made after rolling right (16 steps, matching his jersey number) and tossing the historic pass over three onrushing Cowboys, including Ed "Too Tall" Jones. This game may not have been Montana's best from a statistical point of view, but because this win ushered in the 49ers' dynasty, it also serves as the signature moment to Montana's career, outside of those four Super Bowls, of course.

Getting over the hump against the Cowboys made it even sweeter, for this franchise's playoff hopes had been derailed by Dallas too many times. But the 49ers had made it this far by recording the league's best regular-season record at 13–3 and rallying behind Montana, the NFC's leader in passing efficiency. And so, with this NFC

Championship Game on the line, the 49ers drove 89 yards for the go-ahead touchdown play, with Walsh calling for the "Sprint Right Option" and Montana shaking off the pressure-packed moment to find Clark for "The Catch." It was a breakthrough moment not only for the 49ers, but also Montana, who now would be introduced to a Super Bowl stage that truly bronzed his legacy.

IS JERRY RICE OR JIM BROWN THE NFL'S BEST OF ALL TIME?

 Sure, Joe Montana, Lawrence Taylor, Walter Payton and Johnny Unitas are usually included in any debate over who's the greatest pro football player of all time. But, for much of the past 10–15 years, this argument has centered on whether Jerry Rice or Jim Brown deserves the "greatest" title.

The trick in stating Rice's case is to not simply hail his attributes, but to also pay proper respect to Brown, a phenomenal running back for the Cleveland Browns from 1957–65. While Rice was a consistent threat for most of his 20 seasons, Brown was, too, before abruptly retiring at the peak of his career.

Well, Brown didn't exactly go out on top from a team sense with a Super Bowl confetti shower. Actually, he played in the pre-Super Bowl era, and although his Browns won two Eastern Conference titles—in his rookie year and final season—they lost in subsequent NFL championship games. But the Browns did win an NFL championship in his penultimate season, shutting out the Baltimore Colts 27–0 in 1964. Brown won league MVP awards in his first and final seasons, and although he has only a handful of NFL records, they are remarkable. What's especially jaw dropping are his eight rushing titles, made even more amazing by the fact he got those eight in only nine seasons. He also averaged 5.2 yards per carry, which remains tops among all running backs. But Brown was so much more than records. He had a punishing running style as well as fleet speed that could slice through a secondary. Brown commanded respect; hence his All-Pro selections and Pro Bowl berths in each of his nine pro seasons.

Rice never won a league MVP award, but he was such an integral part in the 49ers' dynasty, and he wonderfully bridged the transition between Montana and Steve Young at quarterback.

Rice has it all when it comes to records, rings, respect and longevity, having retired in 2005 at age 42. He owns over 35 NFL records, including over 10 in the regular season, postseason, and Super Bowl. Most are, of course, receiving marks, including regular-season standards for career yards (22,895), receptions (1,549), and consecutive games with a catch (274).

The most celebrated record Rice owns is touchdowns scored (208). He found the end zone an additional 79 times after passing Brown's 29-year record atop the NFL's all-time list on September 5, 1994. On that season-opening night in 1994, reporters asked Rice if he was the game's best player of all time. Rice declined to pat himself on the back, telling reporters that they could do so for him, if they chose. His team thought so—former 49ers Coach Bill Walsh selected Rice in the first round of the 1985 draft and called him the "greatest player of our time."

Throughout his career, from a 1985 rookie with the 49ers to a final training camp with the Denver Broncos, Rice's work ethic wasn't just legendary, it was inspiring, and something he passed forward to the next generation of NFL stars. Yes, Rice lost one of his records in 2007 when Randy Moss scored 23 touchdowns, but that was still only one better than Rice delivered in 1987, when he played only 12 games.

When he's not relishing in his records, Rice can shine up his three Super Bowl rings, including the one from Super Bowl XXIII in which he was the game's MVP.

Any time you gauge the value of a running back vs. a wide receiver, most times it's an easy call, because running backs touch the ball more often. But it's still not an easy call in this case.

Yes, this is a Bay Area oriented book, but that doesn't preclude us from picking Brown as our winner, which we're doing. Opponents had to game plan around Brown, whereas Rice was one of the 49ers' many weapons of mass destruction. That's no disrespect to Rice, who was an exemplary pro, from his work ethic to his record-breaking statistics. Brown was often described as "a man amongst boys," and 40 years after he retired, the NFL still hasn't seen anyone as dominant in his craft as Brown, our pick as the greatest of all time.

Terrell Owens made four straight trips to the Pro Bowl before concluding his eight-year stint with the 49ers after the 2003 season. But he also made four zillion times as many headlines with controversial acts, including unique celebrations and unsettling comments. We could write a book about his eccentric career. Instead, we'll limit his wild ways to one dubious debate. And you know he had some really off-the-wall moments when the top five don't include those 2002 memories of him moonlighting as a minor league basketball player with the Adirondack Wildcats or celebrating a touchdown with a cheerleader's pompoms during a home loss to the Green Bay Packers.

5. MARCH 16, 2004, PHILLY-BOUND

You just knew he couldn't leave the 49ers without creating drama. And the NFL hadn't seen anything like this. To be fair, Owens' exodus caused more of a stir because of an egregious error by his agent, David Joseph, who missed the deadline to void Owens' contract and thus denied Owens his eagerly awaited shot at free agency. What ensued was part comedy, part legal haggling. The 49ers tried trading him to Baltimore for a second-round draft pick, but Owens blocked that deal, and demanded the NFL step in to mediate the mess. When it was all done, Owens got his wish, ended up with the Philadelphia Eagles, and the 49ers got defensive lineman Brandon Whiting, who played only five games for the 49ers in 2004 before retiring. The Eagles, meanwhile, got to the Super Bowl that season.

4. SEPTEMBER 23, 2003, AT MINNESOTA

Steve Mariucci isn't the only coach Owens verbally chastised. Offensive coordinator Greg Knapp sat on the 49ers bench during a loss at Minnesota when Owens stood in front of him and screamed and hollered. Toddlers couldn't throw a better tantrum. Owens had only five receptions for 55 yards while Minnesota counterpart Randy Moss had eight catches for 172 yards and three touchdowns. Owens' rant came after a failed fourth-down run by Kevan Barlow, and Owens told reporters afterward that his team had "no heart." Owens' motormouth kept revving in that postgame press conference, suggesting that backup Tim Rattay replace Pro Bowl quarterback Jeff Garcia. Owens later apologized to Knapp for his actions, but that visual of a sideline tantrum isn't easy to forget.

3. OCTOBER 31, 2001, AT CHICAGO

Rarely willing to bite his tongue, Owens called out Coach Steve Mariucci after the 49ers blew a 17-point lead and lost in overtime at Chicago. Owens claimed that Mariucci took it easy on too many opponents out of respect for his "buddy system" of fellow coaches. Mariucci called Owens' comments "utterly ridiculous." What was indeed ridiculous was that the 49ers lost that game. Owens hates losing. So losing his cool was to be expected. Or maybe it wasn't this time. After all, the Bears won in overtime when safety Mike Brown returned an interception for a touchdown on a pass that was bobbled by, you guessed it, Mr. Owens.

2. OCTOBER 14, 2002, AT SEATTLE

The "signature moment" of Owens' career came on Monday Night Football at Seattle's Qwest Field. He celebrated his second touchdown by pulling a black Sharpie from his sock, autographing the ball, and handing it to his financial advisor in a field-level, end zone suite. It was original, entertaining, and, of course, self-promoting to the extreme. The 49ers won the game 28–21 to improve to 4–1, and Owens made sure everyone knew he had a big part in that. The Sharpie was in Owens' sock throughout the fourth quarter, and he unsheathed that pen after his 37-yard touchdown catch put the 49ers ahead with about seven and a half minutes remaining.

1. SEPTEMBER 24, 2000, AT DALLAS

Owens' image would never be the same. It wasn't just his two touchdown catches that caused all the fuss during and after a 41–24 win over the host Cowboys. It was how Owens celebrated those scores, twice racing to Dallas' midfield star logo. It was blasphemous, at least in the eyes of the Dallas Cowboys, as well as 49ers officials, who suspended him for a week and fined him $24,000.

In Owens' first sprint to midfield, he posed there by spreading his arms wide and tilting his head skyward toward the hole in Texas Stadium's roof. He initially claimed it was an impromptu act, but later revealed in his autobiography that it was premeditated. When Owens returned to midfield after his second touchdown catch, the Cowboys pursued him, sparking a melee as well as Owens' reputation as a controversial showman.

WHAT WERE T.O.'S TOP FIVE MOMENTS WITH THE 49ERS?

Not everything Terrell Owens did was controversial during his 1996–2003 tenure with the 49ers. In his own immortal words: "Who can make a play? I CAN!" Yes, he did that many times, and let's take a look at which five were his best moments with the 49ers:

5. BARGAIN SHOP

All it took was a late third-round draft pick (89th overall selection) for the 49ers to land Owens, a product of Tennessee-Chattanooga. He averaged 74 receptions, 1,072 yards, and 10 touchdowns in his eight seasons with the 49ers. In the four years after he left, the 49ers didn't have a wide receiver eclipse 70 catches, 750 yards, or six touchdowns. Of course, he also left the 49ers as a much more controversial force than when he arrived as a well-mannered, yes-sir sort in 1996. He wasn't as great of a third-round steal as Montana in 1979, mind you, but finding Owens to complement Rice in the post-John Taylor years was essential to the offense's consistency, and it was a role 1995 first-round pick J.J. Stokes never fulfilled.

4. BLOCK PARTY

Owens once said his fondest memory as a 49ers wasn't a catch or a touchdown but rather the blocks he threw while escorting Garrison Hearst on a 96-yard touchdown run in overtime of the 1998 season-opening win over the Jets. It went down as the longest run in 49ers history, and Owens' willingness to block down field proved critical. He put his chiseled body to good use with that physical presence, and, mind you, this was nearly a decade before he was chiseling his abs by doing situps in his driveway during his Philadelphia Eagles days.

3. T.O. IN OT

Owens not only caught a 17-yard touchdown pass with 17 seconds remaining to force overtime at Atlanta in 2001, he also ended the extra period with a 52-yard touchdown catch. All nine of his receptions (for 183 yards and three touchdowns) came after halftime for the 49ers, who won 37–31. He celebrated his game-clinching touchdown by dunking the football over the Georgia Dome's crossbar. Making the theatrics even better for Owens was that he performed so well in the clutch before an audience that included several family members, who made the drive over from his hometown of Alexander City, Alabama.

2. 20 FOR T.O.

In what was billed as "Jerry Rice Day" in honor of Rice's final home game as a 49er, Owens stole the show and broke an NFL single-game record with 20 receptions. That broke Tom Fears's 50-year-old record. Owens racked up 283 yards, including a 27-yard touchdown catch that sealed the 17–0 win over the Chicago Bears. One of the sidelights to this tale is that, when Rice ended up clearing out his locker at the 49ers' headquarters' in Santa Clara in June 2001, Owens was there to help him. One memento that Rice didn't pack into his car was the game ball from that win over the Bears, and he instead handed it over to Owens.

1. THE CATCH II

Owens dropped four passes before nabbing a clutch, game-winning touchdown catch with three seconds remaining in the 1998 49ers' NFC wild-card win over the Green Bay Packers. The 25-yard play, "Two Jet All Go," lifted the 49ers to a 30–27 home victory, and the play nearly fell apart when quarterback Steve Young stumbled as he backpedaled after the snap. The win also avenged the previous season's loss at Green Bay in the NFC Championship Game, and the moment moved Owens to tears, which he shed on Coach Steve Mariucci's shoulder on the sideline.

No, "The Catch II" didn't reap the illustrious rewards of "The Catch" by Dwight Clark 17 years earlier for the Super Bowl-bound 49ers. Owens' 49ers lost the following week at Atlanta 20–18 in the divisional round, doomed by Hearst's broken ankle. But, hey, Owens' game-winner did prevent the Packers from pursuing their third straight Super Bowl.

95

WHO HAD THE GREATEST RUN IN 49ERS HISTORY?

24. Overtime ended abruptly in the 49ers' 1998 season opener when Garrison Hearst broke loose and fled 96 yards down the right (49ers) sideline for the winning touchdown against the New York Jets. It's the longest run in 49ers history. But is it the best?

Quarterback Steve Young's scramblin'-stumblin' touchdown run against the Minnesota Vikings in 1988 certainly might top Hearst's heroics. With Joe Montana sidelined by back injuries, Young started against the Vikings and delivered his never-say-die, 49-yard jaunt. He eluded seven Vikings (and, officially, the other four) as he zigzagged across Candlestick's field before diving across the goal line.

The 49ers had trailed 21–17 before that third-and-two run with some two minutes remaining. Young instantly gained credibility in the eyes of skeptical 49ers fans who didn't want him threatening Montana's legacy. The 24–21 win also improved the Super Bowl-bound 49ers' record to 6–3, which sure looked a lot better than 5–4. They finished the regular season 10–6, and had they lost the Minnesota game, they would have missed the playoffs with a 9–7 mark.

So epic was Young's mad scramble that Burger King relived it in a 2006 commercial, using computer imaging to replace Young with The King.

The 49ers once had their own "King," a nickname that Hall of Famer Hugh McElhenny wore well from 1952–60 with the 49ers. McElhenny still owns three of the four longest runs in 49ers history, 89- and 82- yarders against the Dallas Texans in 1952, and an 86-yarder against Green Bay in 1956. Old-timers will argue that one of those McElhenny runs trumps Young's or Hearst's.

Hearst's run got a big endorsement shortly after he broke McElhenny's 89-yard club record. Steve Sabol of NFL Films promptly called Hearst's overtime winner the greatest run in league history. *Sports Illustrated*'s Paul Zimmerman vehemently disagreed with Sabol's claim, and Zimmerman countered by offering up Young's 49-yard scramble as his choice for the top run ever. For the purposes of our argument, about who simply had the 49ers' best run, it's Young who breaks away from the pack again and runs past Hearst.

WHO WAS THE 49ERS' SECOND-BEST RECEIVER?

This should be a hotly debated topic, although it may seem a bit silly to argue who's the first runner-up to Jerry Rice in the 49ers' chain of legendary receivers. But consider some of the distinguished candidates: John Taylor, Dwight Clark, Terrell Owens, Gene Washington, Freddie Solomon, Dave Parks, Billy Wilson, and R.C. "Alley Oop" Owens.

Clark and Terrell Owens provided plenty of memorable catches, including, of course, "The Catch" by Clark in the 1981 team's playoff win over the Dallas Cowboys, and "The Catch II" by Owens in the 1997 team's playoff win over the Green Bay Packers.

Clark broke in the same year Joe Montana did with the 49ers, in 1979, and that famous duo began working their magic in Montana's first comeback win, a thriller over New Orleans that same season. Clark went on to make two Pro Bowls before retiring in 1988, the same year the 49ers retired his No. 87 jersey. Twenty years later, he remained the only wide receiver to have his number so honored by the 49ers.

Owens made four Pro Bowls, but those Hawaiian holidays were the least memorable instances of Owens' 49ers days. He was controversial with his celebrations, his blunt comments to the press, and his aloofness in the locker room. The "Catch II" game really did define Owens best. He dropped four passes in that playoff thriller before coming through in the clutch, catching the game-winning touchdown pass in traffic over the middle. Moments later, he was crying on Coach Steve Mariucci's shoulder, showing just how emotional Owens can get. Of course, his big-play ability is also reflected quite well in The Catch II, a catchy moniker but, honestly, not really one Bay Area sports fans really recognize as an all-out nickname. Maybe that's because the 49ers lost the following week. Maybe it's because Owens wore out his welcome here. Maybe it's because nothing can truly be compared to the original Catch by Clark. But it's important not to dismiss Owens' production, as his five 1,000-yard seasons rank second in club annals to Rice's 12.

Before Washington went on to a distinguished career as an NFL executive, he also fared quite well for the 49ers from 1969–77. A Stanford product, he made four straight Pro Bowls from 1969–72. And not to be forgotten is Wilson, who led the league three times in receptions in the 1950s.

Still, it's Taylor who deserves the nod as second-best wide receiver behind Rice, just like when they were teammates from 1987–95. Taylor's most famous catch lifted the 1989 49ers to their third Super Bowl title, as he nabbed Joe

Montana's pass with 34 seconds remaining against the Cincinnati Bengals in Super Bowl XXIII. The following season, Taylor had one of the most memorable Monday Night Football performances, turning short Montana passes into 92- and 95-yard touchdown catches in a comeback win over the Los Angeles Rams.

But go back and read that question carefully.

We didn't ask, who's the second-best wide receiver. We asked who's the second-best receiver.

Because of that terminology, the choice is Roger Craig, the 49ers' former fullback/halfback who played such a vital role in the passing game.

Craig led the 49ers in receiving four times, in 1984, '85, '87, and '88. He capped off that 1984 season by scoring three touchdowns in the 49ers' Super Bowl win over Miami, with two of those touchdowns coming on receptions. In 1985, he became the first player in NFL history to top the 1,000-yard mark both as a runner (1,050) and receiver (1,016), and his 92 catches led the league. He showed just how versatile running backs could be, and Bill Walsh's West Coast offense relied upon Craig's presence to enhance its short passing game. Of course, tight ends also played a pivotal role in the receiving department, as exemplified by the likes of Brent Jones and Russ Francis.

In 1988, Craig's 76 catches for 534 yards complemented his 1,502 rushing yards, and he emerged as the

Associated Press's Offensive Player of the Year. Twenty years later, Craig was enshrined in the Bay Area Sports Hall of Fame. He's still waiting for a call sending him to Canton, Ohio. And perhaps that constant habit of overlooking his credentials is one more reason we're compelled to give him some props here in this debate over Taylor, Terrell Owens, and others.

Once asked to name his top three draft picks of all time, Bill Walsh gave a surprising response: Jerry Rice, Dwight Clark, and Michael Carter. What? NO JOE??!! "Joe goes without saying," replied Walsh, noting that Montana was still the 49ers' "franchise" even 10 years after his trade to Kansas City.

One of the best picks in draft history had to be Walsh's grab of Montana with the last pick of the third round in 1979. He and quarterbacks coach Sam Wyche privately worked out Montana in Los Angeles and, after using their first pick to draft wide receiver James Owens in the second round, they snatched Montana with the number 82 pick overall.

Walsh knew Montana would drop so far after gauging the league's interest in the skinny Notre Dame quarterback. Walsh learned that most teams figured Montana wouldn't be drafted higher than the fifth round—if at all—and might possibly be a Canadian Football League prospect. Green Bay Packers scout Red Cochran urged Packers coach Bart Starr to take Montana earlier in the third round, but Starr instead took Maryland defensive tackle Charlie Johnson, and Cochran then stormed from the draft room.

Also plucked from that 1979 draft was Clark, a 10th-round draft choice who two years later made "The Catch." Clark was discovered when Walsh was scouting Clemson quarterback Steve Fuller.

Walsh drafted Jerry Rice 16th overall in 1985, trading up in the first round to do so. On the eve of a game against the Oilers, Walsh was sitting in his Houston hotel room in 1984 when he flipped on a television, sipped on a margarita, and saw highlights of Rice catching touchdown passes for Mississippi Valley State.

As for Carter, he went from being an Olympic-winning shot putter to a three-time Super Bowl champion. Walsh drafted him in the fifth round of the 1984 draft and Carter served as a staunch nosetackle on the 49ers line for nine seasons.

The 49ers' defense really changed for the better a few years earlier, when Walsh's 1981 draft class produced starting defensive backs Ronnie Lott, Eric Wright, and Carlton Williamson in the first three rounds. That trio made for a tremendous secondary with Dwight Hicks, and that defensive overhaul (including the acquisitions of Fred Dean and Hacksaw Reynolds) was necessary to complement the budding offense.

All of that said, none of the above will go down as Walsh's biggest draft-day coup. Without the magic he worked in 1986, the 49ers might not have gone on to win Super Bowls with their 1988 and '89 teams. The Class of '86 yielded eight starters for those championship runs.

Walsh loved to trade down in the draft, and by fleeing the first round in 1986, that helped him grab wide receiver John Taylor, linebacker/defensive end Charles Haley, fullback Tom Rathman, cornerback Tim McKyer, safety Don Griffin, defensive end Larry Roberts, and offensive linemen Steve Wallace and Kevin Fagan. Even Mel Kiper Jr. has called it the best draft class in NFL history. We certainly agree that the class served as the best drafting by The Genius, Walsh.

WHAT WAS THE 49ERS' WORST TRADE?

When Mike Nolan took over in 2005 as coach and personnel czar of a 2–14 outfit, a flurry of trades ensued and nine players were shipped out in a span of 13 months. The 49ers hadn't traded away that many players since, well, since Bill Walsh also took over a bumbling 2–14 team in 1979. Despite their trigger-happy fingers, neither Nolan nor Walsh can stake claim as having pulled off the worst trade in franchise history.

No, you figure that dubious honor might go to one of the deals that shipped out a big-name 49er who then flourished elsewhere. From Joe Montana to Y.A. Tittle, from Terrell Owens to Jim Plunkett, you can't help but wonder how the 49ers might have been different if those careers had carried on in the Red and Gold.

Let's start with a classic gaffe during Joe Thomas's dismal term as general manager. In 1976, Thomas acquired Plunkett from the New England Patriots for quarterback Tom Owens and first-round draft picks in 1976 and '77. The 49ers released Plunkett after only two seasons, a move that wasn't so shocking until he reappeared as a two-time Super Bowl winner with the Raiders.

Here's another doozey of a trade: Tittle getting dealt in 1961 to the New York Giants. Tittle was 34, but he went on to lead the Giants to three straight NFL championship games. In return for Tittle, the 49ers got lineman Lou Cordileone, who played one year for them before getting traded again to the Los Angeles Rams for defensive end Elbert Kimbrough.

One trade that particularly stung in the wake of the 49ers' 1980s dynasty was a 1992 deal sending Charles Haley to the rival Dallas Cowboys. Fed up with Haley's temper, the 49ers accepted a 1993 second-round pick and a '94 third-round choice for the fierce pass rusher, who promptly won his third, fourth, and fifth Super Bowl rings with Dallas.

One recent nominee for worst trade could be the 2004 case of Owens. Philadelphia Eagles defensive lineman Brandon Whiting is who the 49ers got in return for Owens in a convoluted three-way deal with Baltimore and Philadelphia. The trade's jumbled mess stemmed from Owens' failure to void his contract in time to become a free agent, and then his refusal to report to Baltimore in an original two-team deal. As for Whiting, well, he had no sacks in his five games as a 49er before heading off into retirement.

Even though Montana proved worthy of a first-round draft pick, the 49ers didn't have one available back in 1979. That, ladies and gentlemen, is courtesy of what indeed ranks as the worst trade in their history. To acquire running back O.J. Simpson and his wounded knees in

1978, the 49ers shipped five draft picks to the Buffalo Bills, including a first-round choice in 1979, second-round picks in '78 and '79, a third-rounder in 1978, and a fourth-rounder in 1979.

Simpson was only five years removed from one of the finest seasons ever by a running back, having rushed for 2,003 yards in the 1973 season's 14-game slate. But Simpson played only two seasons in his native San Francisco before retiring because of those arthritic knees. He then went on to a life of...oh, we don't need to rehash that, do we? Come to think of it, let's stop rehashing that trade also. Who needs the lousy memories?

WHAT WAS THE 49ERS' BIGGEST INNOVATION FOR THE NFL?

Bill Walsh's West Coast offense isn't the only innovation the 49ers have given to the NFL. The 49ers also brought you:

THE SHOTGUN SNAP

Coach Red Hickey surprised the Colts in 1960 by having his quarterback line up about five yards behind the center. The 49ers used three quarterbacks—Y.A. Tittle, John Brodie, and Bob Waters—to top the Colts 30–22. When Hickey resigned in 1963, the shotgun also disappeared from the 49ers offense, though it reemerged with Jeff Garcia lining up in it in 2001.

THE "FRIDGE"

Okay, William "The Refrigerator" Perry didn't play for the 49ers, but he gained his fame by diving into the end zone on a 1984 gimmick the 49ers introduced with guard Guy McIntyre. Walsh used McIntyre as a blocking back in short-yardage situations, and by doing so with success against the Bears in the 1984 season's NFC Championship Game, it led to Perry moonlighting in a similar role in 1985.

THE ALLEY-OOP

When R.C. Owens had two touchdown catches off lobbed passes in a 1957 win over the Los Angeles Rams, the "Alley-Oop" was born. It also led to a dramatic winning touchdown catch by Owens in a midseason win over Detroit.

CEREMONIAL CONTRACTS

Roger Craig wanted to retire as a 49er, so he showed up at training camp in 1994 and signed a one-day deal worth $0. Others who've also signed ceremonial contracts: Jerry Rice (49ers), Tim Brown (Raiders), Emmitt Smith (Cowboys), Art Monk (Redskins), Dorsey Levens (Packers), Leonard Marshall (Giants), Randall Cunningham (Eagles), and Duce Staley (Eagles).

WALSH'S SYSTEM

So it's clear that the West Coast offense wasn't the only innovation. However, it was the best.

Employing multiple weapons in a horizontal passing game replete with short- and medium-range throws has been adopted throughout much of the NFL in the past 20 years. The 49ers ran a version of it all the way up to the Dennis Erickson era in 2004–05.

Mike Shanahan's Broncos, Mike Holmgren's Packers, and Jon Gruden's Buccaneers won Super Bowls employing much of Walsh's West Coast philosophies, while others who reached the Super Bowl included Andy Reid's Philadelphia Eagles and Holmgren's Seahawks.

Walsh's West Coast philosophy was cutting edge, and it cut apart defenses little by little until the 49ers had piled up enough yards and points to squash the opposition. Al Davis' beloved vertical attack this wasn't. Instead, Walsh's scheme consisted of two-back formations, perfectly timed routes, touch passes, plenty of motion, and a horizontally oriented style that attacked 3–4 defensive schemes. Fullbacks and tight ends also played pivotal roles, breaking free of their blocking duties to become full-fledged receivers. Joe Montana's mechanics, footwork, vision, instincts, and calmness fit perfectly into Walsh's system, one that Steve Young successfully adapted to when he replaced Montana. Sure, there were some long pass plays, but they usually came on short passes that receivers stretched into big gains, or yards after the catch (YAC, a term that became part of the 49er fans' vocabulary as it associated to great ones like Jerry Rice and John Taylor).

For 25 years, many teams culled some variation off Walsh's system. And while the West Coast's popularity has waned in favor of spread formations (see: those run by Peyton Manning and Tom Brady), Walsh's scheme will forever be remembered as a major pioneer to the NFL's offensive boom.

WHAT'S THE BEST BRANCH ON THE BILL WALSH COACHING TREE?

When Bill Walsh died in July 2007 after battling leukemia, 21 of the NFL's 32 teams had a head coach linked to Walsh. Other than Seattle's Mike Holmgren—Walsh's offensive coordinator from 1986–88—the coaches weren't direct descendants of Walsh but were two or three degrees of separation from him.

Here's how it breaks down: the tree includes 40 head coaches, initially branching out with eight who immediately served under him: Dennis Green (Vikings, Cardinals), Holmgren (Packers, Seahawks), George Seifert (49ers, Panthers), Sam Wyche (Bengals, Buccaneers), Ray Rhodes (Eagles, Packers), Mike White (Raiders), Bruce Coslet (Jets, Bengals), and Chuck Studley (Oilers). The only Super Bowl winners out of those eight direct descendants are Holmgren (Green Bay, 1996) and Seifert, who succeeded Walsh and led the 49ers' 1989 and '94 teams to Lombardi trophies.

Holmgren's wing is impressive: his descendants include Steve Mariucci, Andy Reid, Marty Mornhinweg, Dick Jauron, Brad Childress, Jim Mora, Mike Sherman, and Jim Zorn. Two-time Super Bowl winner Mike Shanahan falls under Seifert's branch, as does Pete Carroll, Jeff Fisher, Gary Kubiak, and Gregg Williams.

Another strong branch can be seen in Rhodes, who's produced a Super Bowl winner in Jon Gruden (Buccaneers, 2002), as well as Sean Payton, Mike McCarthy, Joe Vitt, and Bill Callahan.

Of all the coaches who have branched out of Bill Walsh's coaching tree, however, Dennis Green has spawned off the most impressive list of other coaches. In addition, Green, a minority, stands as a symbol of Walsh's legacy of diversity, the elder statesman having started the Minority Coaches Fellowship in 1987.

Green coached under Walsh at Stanford in 1977–78, then coached wide receivers with the 49ers in 1979 and 1986–88. Two of Green's former assistants at Minnesota went on to win Super Bowls, Brian Billick (Baltimore, 2000), and Tony Dungy (Indy, 2006). Others under Green's side of the tree: Mike Tice, Marvin Lewis, Mike Nolan, Jack Del Rio, Scott Linehan, Lovie Smith, Rod Marinelli, Mike Tomlin, Herm Edwards, and Mike Smith.

"Clearly, this modern game that we now play came on the footsteps of Bill Walsh and the many coaches that he influenced," Green said in a 2006 conference call with Bay Area media. "If you look at the offenses that we are now using and everything that has taken place from the West Coast, Bill Walsh was an instrumental part of that. Also, he gave all those guys a chance to grow."

WHO WAS THE 49ERS' BIGGEST DRAFT BUST?

As the only number one overall draft pick in 49ers history, quarterback Alex Smith will either thrive or fail, meaning he'll be the second coming of Joe Montana or the franchise's biggest draft bust. But considering he's only been on the job since midway through his 2005 rookie season, it's too early to determine Smith's payoff for the 49ers.

Other viable contenders include defensive tackle Reggie McGrew and wide receivers Rashaun Woods and J.J. Stokes. McGrew, the 49ers' number one pick in 1999, struggled with injuries throughout his career before the 49ers finally gave up after three seasons. Stokes's career wasn't as bad as you might think. But it probably seems that way considering the 49ers moved up to draft him 10th overall in 1995 and he never became the next Jerry Rice (as if anyone could.)

As for Woods, the 31st overall pick in 2004, he barely played in his two seasons with the 49ers, as injuries and a questioned passion for the game doomed him. He only produced seven catches for 160 yards and one touchdown, all in his rookie year. He spent 2005 on injured reserve and got traded in 2006 to the Chargers, who promptly cut him in training camp.

And before you throw Lawrence Phillips into the mix, remember that the St. Louis Rams drafted him, not the 49ers. That said, signing Phillips in 1999 turned out to be a fateful move for the 49ers, as he missed the block on a blitzing Aeneas Williams that led to Steve Young's career-ending concussion.

But it's none of these choices. Actually, it's another 49ers quarterback who currently holds the title of biggest draft bust. Who is it? Druckenmiller. No need for his first name (Jim). Any mention of Druckenmiller and 49ers fans will let out a groan. Druck was the 26th overall pick out of Virginia Tech in 1997, and rather than become Young's successor, he got a quick ticket out of the NFL. He played in only six games, with that big arm of his completing 21 of 52 passes with one touchdown and four interceptions. He struggled to read defenses, move in the pocket, grasp the 49ers' West Coast system, and pass accurately. Bill Walsh advised the 49ers to instead draft Jake Plummer, but what did Walsh ever know about quarterbacks?

Even though the 49ers won in Druckenmiller's debut—a relief appearance in the 1997 season opener at St. Louis—he posted a lowly 19.3 passer rating, throwing three interceptions, and completing only 10 of 28 passes for 108 yards and a touchdown. The 49ers traded him to Miami in 1999 for a seventh-round pick, but he never played there, and soon the prototypical, big-arm gunslinger was scraping around in the XFL and Arena

League. Of course, other first-round quarterbacks failed with other franchises, but the 49ers are notorious for churning out superstar quarterbacks, and when one fails like Druckenmiller (and possibly Smith), then that wart stands out above all others.

WHICH 49ER IS MOST OVERDUE FOR THE HALL OF FAME?

Defensive end Fred Dean, who helped ignite the 49ers' 1980s dynasty, finally received his long-awaited invitation to the Pro Football Hall of Fame on February 2, 2008. So who's up next in the 49ers' chorus line of superstars?

One piece of the 49ers' dynasty was certainly running back/fullback Roger Craig, who's been overlooked by Hall of Fame voters despite being a pioneer as well as the versatile back needed for Walsh's West Coast offense.

Craig became the first running back to total 1,000 yards both rushing and receiving in the same season, doing so in 1985. Only Marshall Faulk has accomplished that feat since then, doing so in 1999.

Odd as it might seem, no 49ers lineman from any of their five Super Bowl teams is enshrined in Canton. Their offensive line was more of a serviceable unit than an All-Star squadron, although their coach, Bobb McKittrick, worked wonders instituting what some considered controversial blocking techniques. McKittrick himself deserves a spot in the Hall of Fame if voters ever recognize assistant coaches who've made an undeniable impact on the sport.

Guard/center Randy Cross made three Pro Bowls and remains fresh in people's minds thanks to his stellar work as a broadcaster. Guy McIntyre made five straight Pro Bowls for the 49ers from 1989–93. Go way back to the 49ers' inception and you'll find another Hall contender in quarterback John Brodie, who was a two-time Pro Bowl player but also a franchise institution from 1957–73.

Although Dean received his long-awaited invitation to the Hall, another pass-rushing feign deserves entry, that being Charles Haley. He last played in 1999—a playoff cameo for the 49ers—and he was the first player to win five Super Bowl rings, the first two coming with the 1988 and '89 49ers. As for Haley's other three rings, we won't talk about those, unless you really want to relive the trade that sent him to a Dallas Cowboys dynasty that won three Super Bowls in four years between 1992–95. Haley has one hundred and a half sacks and five Pro Bowl leis in his closet, representing the 49ers in Hawaii in 1988, '90, and '91.

Haley made the Pro Football Hall of Fame's list of 26 semifinalists for the 2008 enshrinement ceremony. But, alas, his entry was blocked, something offensive linemen failed to do so often during his storied career.

Yes, the 49ers have had great players over the past several decades. But imagine if their Super Bowl dynasty never happened, a dark image that would have occurred if Eddie DeBartolo Jr. didn't take over as owner in 1977. He triumphantly reigned over the 49ers for just over 20 years

117

before exiting the NFL scene, a result of a Louisiana gambling-license scandal.

Eddie D.—or Mr. D, if you prefer, or Mr. DeBartolo, as ex-players respectfully salute him—was the kingpin of the 49ers' unparalleled stretch of five Lombardi Trophies in 14 seasons, from 1981 to 1994. His greatest move was hiring Bill Walsh as coach in 1979, and the 49ers turned into the NFL's version of "Camelot," where so many players desperately wanted to come for what annually was a legitimate Super Bowl chance. DeBartolo demanded success, and when his team failed to meet his high expectations, he challenged not only his coaches, but his star players. Hall of Fame defensive back Ronnie Lott remembers DeBartolo once asking him after a defeat, "What was that about?" Lott also hasn't forgotten how DeBartolo lavished luxuries on the team, such as traveling in a first-class manner, bringing in top entertainers for off-field functions and once flying team members and their families to Hawaii after a Super Bowl victory.

DeBartolo may have stepped down as the 49ers principal owner in sour fashion—he received a one-year suspension from the league—but it's not as if he committed any gambling sin like betting on his sport or team, a la Pete Rose.

DeBartolo was inducted in April 2008 into the Bay Area Sports Hall of Fame, which created the category of "Distinguished Achievement" to welcome him to their club. All the A-list stars came out for the honor, including Joe Montana, Jerry Rice, and Lott, who pleaded with the media to spur on DeBartolo's induction into Canton's sacred hall.

"He accomplished what a lot of owners wish they could, and he's done that five times over," Montana said before DeBartolo's BASHOF induction.

Said Lott: "Here's a gentleman that has five (Super Bowl titles) and he really defines what ownership is about, especially in this modern era. If you look at Mark Cuban and other maverick-type owners, they want to be like him. They treat their players the way Mr. DeBartolo treated us."

Rice added: "What he did for the NFL, having a dynasty and having a team that represented the NFL the right way with a lot of character, I think it's time."

We agree. It's time Eddie D. gets a bronze bust of himself in his native Ohio.

IS LOTT'S PINKIE THE MOST UNBELIEVABLE SACRIFICE EVER?

Ronnie Lott owns four Super Bowl rings from his 49ers career, but the best symbol of Lott's championship presence is his left pinkie. Well, what's left of it. He had the tip of that finger amputated so he could play in the 1985 season's playoffs.

Is it the most famous sacrifice of a body part in Bay Area sports history? What about former Giants pitcher Dave Dravecky's left arm, which he broke—and later had amputated—while attempting a comeback from cancer? That took place in 1989, with his arm shattering as he made a pitch at Montreal's Olympic Stadium.

What about former Raiders center Jim Otto's entire body? He had his right leg amputated in 2007, one of some 50 surgeries he's endured, including several on his knees and shoulders?

What about 49ers defensive lineman Bryant Young playing with a 16-inch rod in his right leg for the final nine of his 14 seasons?

What about Bob St. Clair, another former 49ers lineman, losing five teeth while blocking a punt in the 1950s?

What about all those other athletes who've played hurt with concussions, torn ligaments, and broken bones? What about Lott? How does he explain his pinkie to his children? Tears welled up in his eyes when he was asked that question during a 2003 press conference announcing the 49ers' retirement of his No. 42.

"My kids right now, for all they know, it looks like E.T.'s head. But at some point they'll get it," Lott said. "That's what I'm hoping, that at some point in their lives, they'll be able to make sacrifices for their teammates, for their friends. It's kind of hard to get people to understand why would you do that.... At the end of the day, it's all worth it."

"We were fortunate to have all these players, but Ronnie was the best defensive back to have ever played the game," former 49ers coach Bill Walsh said years ago. "You can tell how important (his amputated pinkie) is to him, how much passion for the game means to him."

That attitude, that leadership, that team-first loyalty is what helped make Lott a Hall of Famer. Okay, that and some bone-crushing hits, no pun intended regarding his pinkie, which is our choice as the ultimate symbol of team sacrifice.

SHOULD THE 49ERS HAVE KEPT JEFF GARCIA?

 33 Quarterback Jeff Garcia's release in March 2004 stands as a key flashpoint in the 49ers' downward turn this millennium. They shouldn't have cut ties with him, and they've paid the consequences for that—and many other boneheaded moves—since 2004.

Garcia was the 49ers' full-time starter from 2000–2003, making three Pro Bowls in the process and leading the 2002 team to the second-biggest comeback in NFL playoff history, a 39–38 triumph over the New York Giants in wild-card action. In the four years following his departure, the 49ers used seven different starting quarterbacks: Tim Rattay, Ken Dorsey, Cody Pickett, Alex Smith, Trent Dilfer, Shaun Hill, and Chris Weinke.

Garcia certainly wasn't flawless. Fans despised his "happy feet." But he had the grit, passion, and talent the 49ers needed from that position once Steve Young retired. And Garcia, who grew up a 49ers fan in nearby Gilroy, knew just how sacred Young and Montana made the 49ers quarterback throne.

He played with a chip on his shoulder, and still does, having bounced from the 49ers to Cleveland, Detroit,

Philadelphia, and Tampa Bay. Adding to that chip was his foolish release by the 49ers in 2004. He was part of a devastating purge of seven offensive starters: Garcia, running back Garrison Hearst, wide receivers Terrell Owens and Tai Streets, offensive linemen Derrick Deese and Ron Stone, and tight end Jed Weaver.

The 49ers have followed up with some of the worst offensive outputs in their franchise's 58-year history. Could Garcia alone have prevented that? No. There was just too much widespread damage done by that 2004 clear cutting of the roster, something that happened under Terry Donahue's dismal watch as the 49ers general manager.

Although Garcia was released by the 49ers about a month and a half after his highly publicized drunken-driving arrest, both sides said he got dumped for salary-cap reasons. Garcia was slated to earn a $500,000 roster bonus and make almost $10 million in base salary in 2004. The 49ers failed to renegotiate his contract, so they cut him, even though he still accounted for $10 million in their 2004 salary cap.

Looking back, John York should have forked over more dough to keep Garcia, as it still would have been cheaper than the alternative. One year later, the 49ers had to guarantee a then-record $24 million to first-round draft pick Alex Smith, who signed a six-year, $36 million pact.

Garcia eventually escaped the quarterback graveyards in Cleveland and Detroit to revive his career in

Philadelphia. He replaced an injured Donovan McNabb and even led the 2006 Eagles to a playoff win over the same Giants franchise he beat four years earlier in that epic 49ers comeback. In 2007, Garcia was in the playoffs again, this time with the Tampa Bay Buccaneers, who lost their wild-card game to the eventual Super Bowl-champion Giants. The 49ers, meanwhile, were stuck debating whether Smith and Coach Mike Nolan could reconcile the feud that erupted during a woeful 5–11 season. Once spring rolled around, Nolan declared it an open competition at quarterback between Smith, Hill, and J.T. O'Sullivan. Oh the travesty of a tragically dull quarterback controversy. It would have been so much easier had Garcia not been ushered out of 4949 Centennial Blvd.

ARE THE 49ERS STILL THE BAY AREA'S MOST POPULAR TEAM?

34 No pro team has won more championships in the Bay Area than the 49ers with five. But their last Lombardi leap was way back on January 29, 1995. Since then, the 49ers have fallen to the back of the parity-driven pack. Not only did they go five straight seasons without a playoff berth from 2003–07, they posted five straight losing seasons for the first time in the franchise's 62-year history.

The Bay Area does have its share of loyal fans, and the 49ers recently built a marketing campaign around their "Faithful." But the Bay Area also has plenty of frontrunners, too, and that means if any of the other teams were to get on a hot streak, the door is wide open to cut into the 49ers' once impenetrable popularity.

The Warriors certainly created a buzz in the spring of 2007 with their first playoff appearance in 13 years. Celebrities turned out courtside, Oracle Arena set attendance records with over 20,000 fans at some games, and there were points being scored at a rapid clip. More of the same followed in a riveting 2007–08 season by an improved Warriors squad. But there would be no playoff encore as they just missed landing the Western Conference's No. 8 seed.

Scoring points and thrilling fans is what the 49ers used to do. But once 2003 hit, their offensive playcard looked more like a last will and testament. The 49ers became boring, and, hence the arrival of Mike Martz to coordinate the 2008 offense.

Their 2007 club spent much of the season threatening to set several franchise records for offensive futility. First-year offensive coordinator Jim Hostler—the third OC in as many seasons under Coach Mike Nolan—took the brunt of the criticism early on and wasn't fired until season's end.

Yet through it all, the 49ers remain popular, helped immensely by the inability of the region's other teams to consistently put out a winning product. Despite the 2007 club's 5–11 record, the 49ers kept alive a home sellout streak that dates back to 1981. Sellouts will be a rarity for the Giants and A's as they go through what's expected to be a painful rebuilding process over the next couple of years. Although the Warriors and Sharks have the makings of serious playoff contenders for years to come, pro football still rules the Bay Area market. If the 49ers and Raiders didn't have eight Lombardi trophies combined, they might only draw headlines during the season. Instead, anything written about them results in "most viewed" billing on newspaper websites. And because the 49ers have stood out longer as the Bay Area's most popular team, the shelf life of that title has yet to expire.

WHO MADE A GREATER IMPACT ON PRO FOOTBALL, AL DAVIS OR BILL WALSH?

Al Davis has spent nearly 50 years in pro football. And we mean IN pro football. He lives and breathes the sport, especially his Raiders.

His accomplishments over the decades can't be dismissed, no matter how overshadowed they've become by his "maverick" reputation and his increasing amount of franchise-foiling moves.

Another remarkable legacy belongs to Bill Walsh, one filled with Super Bowl wins, a dynamic offensive scheme, and a push for more minority coaches. Walsh turned around the 49ers' franchise shortly upon his hiring in 1979. He won three Super Bowls in his 10 seasons. While he assisted the 49ers in future years as a general manager and consultant, Walsh's legacy continues to have a trickledown effect throughout the NFL. His West Coast offense has served as a staple for many teams' playbook, a result of the extensive tree that has sprung up with coaches who are one, two, or three degrees of separation away from Walsh, who passed away in 2007. (See: Argument number 28.)

Walsh's methods extended far beyond his pioneering system. It was how he implemented things, how he ran practices, how he scripted plays to start games, how he jockeyed down the draft board, and how he cut loose players a year too early rather than a year too late. The NFL is known as a copycat league, and so many coaches have attempted to duplicate Walsh's methods.

Both Walsh and Davis can be described as pioneers, innovators, and true icons. Davis is the one who actually gave Walsh his first pro gig in 1966 as the Raiders' running backs coach.

A few years earlier, Davis joined the Raiders as their head coach and general manager at age 33. That was in 1963, after the Raiders had struggled in their first three years of existence. He immediately jump-started the franchise, inheriting a 1–13 team and turning it into a 10–4 winner, the largest single-season turnaround in pro football history.

Of Davis' storied legacy and his "commitment to excellence," he should be especially proud of being at the forefront of racial integration, and, for that matter, the overall diversification in pro football. He hired the first black coach (Art Shell), the first Hispanic coach (Tom Flores), and the first female chief executive (Amy Trask). Carrying over from his early days as a San Diego Chargers assistant, Davis also believed in the black player, no matter their position or college. His stance as an equal-opportunity employer didn't stop there. Davis gave renegades new life, so long as they could play the game and win.

It's no mistake he's in the Pro Football Hall of Fame, and it's no coincidence that he's presented nine of former Raiders at their induction into Canton, the latest being coach John Madden in 2006. When Davis walked off the enshrinement stage in 2006 and was asked about Warren Moon becoming the first black quarterback inducted, Davis dared one reporter to name any organization that's done more for racial diversity than the Raiders.

Davis also played a key role in keeping the games going. He not only helped forge the American Football League's merger with the NFL, but he also has brokered peace in ratifying new collective bargaining agreements, including the 2006 deal. He, of course, hasn't been afraid to challenge the NFL establishment, as obviously evident during the Raiders' move to Los Angeles and their quest for a new stadium there.

His legacy has taken a beating in recent years, through his flurry of coaching moves, flexing of authority, and questionable personnel moves (e.g., trading away Randy Moss in 2007 and signing overpriced free agents in March 2008). But you have to look at the lifetime of work Davis has contributed to the NFL. That's what we did, and we've concluded he's had a bigger impact than Walsh.

WHICH RAIDERS SEASON WAS THE BEST?

First of all, you can't be considered the franchise's best team ever if you didn't win a championship in your final game. Can you?

Former Raiders coach John Madden disagrees, saying his 1977 Raiders are the franchise's all-time best team, at least on one victorious Sunday in Pittsburgh. Madden's team, the reigning Super Bowl champions, beat the rival Steelers and improved to 2–0. But that game took a physical toll on the Raiders, who went 11–3 in the regular season and bowed out of the playoffs with an AFC Championship Game loss at Denver.

If Madden thinks so strongly that was the Raiders' best team, he certainly has had a good vantage point. We'll just rephrase the question to: Which Raiders' season was their best?

The 2002 offensive juggernaut got shipwrecked by the Buccaneers in Super Bowl XXXVII. The 1967 team went 13–1, then won the American Football League championship, but then lost to Vince Lombardi's Green Bay Packers 33–14 in Super Bowl II. Al Davis apparently thought his 1983 club was the best of the best. After those "Los Angeles" Raiders clobbered the Washington Redskins 38–9 in Super Bowl XVIII, Davis announced they were the Raiders' best team of all time and could challenge any team from any era.

When an NFL Films panel disagreed and placed a number 20 ranking on the 1983 Raiders during a series about great Super Bowl teams, the Raiders issued a press release condemning the NFL Films' designation. Tom Flores, coach of that 1983 team, said the 20th ranking was ridiculous and his squad deserved top-three consideration. The 1983 Raiders included 14 players who at one time were a Pro Bowl selection, including Marcus Allen, whose 74-yard touchdown run will live forever on Super Bowl highlight reels.

We also have to consider the 1980 Raiders. They were pioneers and deserve special kudos for that. They became the first wild-card entry to win a Super Bowl. Quarterback Jim Plunkett didn't make costly mistakes, and the Raiders took advantage of the ones the Eagles made, including three interceptions by Rod Martin in the 27–10 win in Super Bowl XV. On the way there, the Raiders won playoff games at Cleveland and rival San Diego. What a way to cap off a season that started 2–3 and included quarterback Dan Pastorini going down with a broken leg.

Atop the Raiders' rankings, however, should be the 1976 breakthrough team, coached by Madden and quarterbacked by Ken Stabler. That Super Bowl-winning group went 13–1 in the regular season, with the lone loss coming in Week Four at New England in the midst of a brutal stretch of five straight road games. The Raiders avenged that loss by topping the Patriots 24–21 to open the playoffs, and then after knocking off longtime nemesis Pittsburgh 24–7 in the AFC Championship Game, the Raiders creamed the Minnesota Vikings 32–14 in Super Bowl XI.

That team certified the Raiders as an elite franchise, and it showcased Hall of Famers in Madden, wide receiver Fred Biletnikoff, cornerback Willie Brown, linebacker Ted Hendricks, guard Gene Upshaw, offensive tackle Art Shell, as well as the big man upstairs, Al Davis.

The Raiders' mission isn't to get the most busts into Canton, however. It's to get the most Super Bowl trophies into their clutches, and it all started with a very impressive run to that crown in 1976.

WHO HAD THE RAIDERS' BEST SINGLE-SEASON EFFORT?

 37 During the 2007 summer, the Raiders issued a press release because they felt so disrespected by a NFL Network series on the top 10 single-season performances in league history. The Raiders were excluded from that list entirely, so they offered their own top four. But that's not enough for us. We're thirsty for a six-pack, and let's pop these open:

6. ART POWELL, 1963

The Raiders excluded this from their honor roll, but we didn't. Al Davis considers Powell "the Terrell Owens of his era," and Davis means that in terms of on-field dominance. Powell had 16 touchdown catches in the 14-game season, and that still stands as the single-season franchise record.

5. BO KNOWS, 1987

Okay, another oversight by the Raiders, but not us. This was Bo Jackson's first year in the NFL, although he only played seven games after completing his baseball duties with the Kansas City Royals. Jackson averaged a franchise-record 6.8 yards per carry, a mark that would remain an impressive 5.8 per carry average if you took away his epic 91-yard run into a Seattle Kingdome tunnel during a 221-yard effort on Monday Night Football.

4. 11 ANGRY MEN, 1967

The Raiders defense racked up 67 sacks, which stands as the all-time AFL record and the most in pro football history before the 16-game schedule took effect. To compare, the NFL record stands at 72, set by the 1984 Chicago Bears in, yes, a 16-game campaign.

3. RICH GANNON, 2002

As the Raiders' first NFL MVP since Marcus Allen in 1985, Gannon's year included a league-high and franchise-record 4,689 yards passing. He had 10 300-yard games, and he completed 67.6 percent of his passes for a Raiders record. His season came to a crashing halt, however, in the Super Bowl, where he had five passes intercepted, three of which were returned for touchdowns in the Bucs' 48–21 rout in San Diego.

2. LESTER HAYES, 1980

His 13 interceptions in that regular season remain the most in NFL history since Dick "Night Train" Lane's 14 in 1952. More incredible were Hayes's additional five interceptions in a postseason that led to a Super Bowl XV triumph. He was the AP's Defensive Player of the Year, and someday

Hayes might make it into the Pro Football Hall of Fame based in large part on 1980.

1. GEORGE BLANDA, 1970

The Raiders call it the best single-season performance in pro football history, and Blanda certainly does have a strong case. Blanda came off the bench to save the Raiders from defeat in five straight games. He provided either a clutch touchdown pass or a field goal in the final seconds for four wins and a tie. During the pandemonium after a game-winning field goal against Cleveland, play-by-play voice Bill King shouted: "George Blanda has just been elected king of the world." Later that year, Blanda, at age 43, became the oldest quarterback to play in a title game, throwing two touchdown passes and kicking a field goal in a 27–17 loss in the AFC final.

BIGGER RAIDERS NIGHTMARE: IMMACULATE RECEPTION OR TUCK RULE?

Google the terms "Immaculate Reception" and "Tuck Rule Game" and, bam, they've got their own Wikipedia references. Thus, the Raiders' most painful plays indeed are immortalized.

But can the "Tuck Rule" controversy match the pain inflicted 30 years earlier by the "Immaculate Reception?"

First off, the details on the Tuck Rule. Before the 2001 game against the Patriots, this rule—regarding a quarterback pumping the ball before an attempted pass—was unknown to nearly everyone.

On the play, the 2001 Raiders thought they iced their 13–10 lead in the final two minutes when blitzing cornerback Charles Woodson sacked Patriots quarterback Tom Brady near midfield and forced a fumble (or, a supposed fumble, in this case) that linebacker Greg Biekert recovered.

A replay review ensued, the play was reversed, an incompletion was ruled and, five plays later, Adam Vinatieri began his clutch-kicking legacy with a game-tying, 45-yard field goal through snow showers. Overtime followed, the Raiders never touched the ball and Vinatieri won it on a 23-yard field goal.

The Patriots went on to capture their first Super Bowl. The Raiders went on to the Super Bowl, too, albeit a year later and without Coach Jon Gruden, who was on the opposing sideline for the Tampa Bay Buccaneers in a rout of the Raiders in Super Bowl XXXVII.

And now we must relive the "Immaculate Reception," as it so often is in NFL Films replays and in the minds of the Raider Nation. The 1972 Raiders were playing an AFC divisional playoff game when one play turned the fortunes of the Pittsburgh Steelers. The play: Oakland saw its 7–6 lead disappear when the Steelers converted a fourth-and-10 play into a 60-yard touchdown "reception" by Franco Harris, who scooped up Terry Bradshaw's pass that "nearly" hit the ground after it bounced off John "Frenchy" Fuqua when he got hit by Raiders safety Jack Tatum. Did the ball really bounce off Fuqua, or off Tatum? Was it legal? Well, it was a touchdown that the Raiders—and Steelers— never will forget.

Making the Immaculate Reception so much tougher to digest is the finality that accompanied it. Just like that, the Raiders' season had ended. Well, it did once the referees made their delayed ruling and once fans retreated from the field so the extra-point kick could cap the 13–7 result. As devastating as the Tuck Rule was, those Raiders at least had some plays to try saving their season.

It took four years for the Raiders to rebound from the Immaculate Reception and make the Super Bowl. It may take another four generations for the Raiders to forget that play, however—and that's why we give it the honor of biggest Raiders nightmare.

WHICH HEISMAN WINNER MADE THE BEST OAKLAND RAIDER?

Jim Plunkett has two Super Bowl rings he won with the Raiders. Tim Brown dominates the Raiders record books. So which Heisman Trophy winner worked out best for the Raiders? Or should the debate also include Marcus Allen, Charles Woodson, Bo Jackson, Desmond Howard, and Billy Cannon, the Raiders' other Heisman winners?

Before you argue that Allen, a Hall of Famer, or Jackson, a multi-sport star, were better Heisman winners-turned-Raiders, keep in mind these debates are about the Bay Area, and both Allen and Jackson played their entire Raiders careers with the Los Angeles version.

Now, if you wanted to expand the debate to include all Raiders, then Allen would get the nod. He was the first player in NFL history with 10,000 rushing yards and 5,000 receiving yards, and he won MVP honors in the Raiders' Super Bowl XVIII win. Allen is also the Raiders' all-time leading rusher in terms of attempts, yards, and touchdowns. He played for the Raiders from 1982–91, then fled Al Davis' doghouse and finished his career with the Kansas City Chiefs.

Jackson was drafted by the Raiders in 1987, and he promptly reeled off the two longest runs in Raiders history, 92 yards in 1989 against Cincy and 91 yards as a rookie when he ran out of Seattle's Kingdome. The last Heisman winner drafted by the Raiders is Woodson, a cornerback who made the Pro Bowl his first four seasons out of Michigan. But Woodson's work ethic and production slacked off, and he managed only one interception in five of his eight seasons in Oakland before reviving his career in Green Bay.

Two other Heisman winners the Raiders acquired were Howard, a respectable return man for the 1997–98 Raiders, and Cannon, who won the '59 Heisman as a running back and became a great receiving tight end with the Raiders from 1964–69.

Still, this debate is pretty much a two-man show between Plunkett and Brown,

The Plunkett Reclamation Project is unparalleled. After winning the Heisman in 1970 at Stanford, Plunkett got drafted number one overall by the New England Patriots, who traded him in 1976 to the 49ers. Plunkett threw 22 touchdowns and 30 interceptions in two seasons for the 49ers, who cut him loose before 1978. No team claimed him off waivers and the Raiders signed him as a free agent. Plunkett replaced an injured Dan Pastorini during the 1980 season, led the Raiders to a wild-card berth and all way through to a Super Bowl XV win over Philadelphia. Plunkett was that Super Bowl's MVP, and three years later, he was in the Super Bowl again, this time quarterbacking the Raiders past the Washington Redskins 38–9.

And what about Brown? No player had a longer tenure in the Silver and Black than Brown, whose 16 seasons (1988–2003) trumped by one year the career of center Jim Otto. Longevity isn't all the Raiders got from their 1988 first-round draft pick out of Notre Dame.

Brown is their all-time leader in receptions (1,070), receiving yards (14,734), and overall touchdowns (104). He led the league in kickoff returns as a rookie, also put in plenty of time as a punt returner, made nine Pro Bowls, and helped the 2002 Raiders into the Super Bowl.

But, again, Plunkett won two Super Bowls. And he epitomized how the Raiders are willing to give wayward players an opportunity to salvage their careers, all in hopes of, well, just winning, baby.

WHO'S THE RAIDERS' BIGGEST DRAFT BUST SINCE 1995?

As the NFL draft's number one overall pick in 2007, quarterback JaMarcus Russell is either going to have a boom or bust career. That's how most first-round picks are judged, and the Raiders have had their share of busts since returning to Oakland in 1995.

But the saddest story among all their first-round draft picks is undoubtedly the tragic case of defensive tackle Darrell Russell. His career started out promisingly after being selected number two overall. But before he could build on two Pro Bowl berths, Russell's career was derailed by substance abuse problems. He served two suspensions for violating the league's drug policy, and the Raiders cast him aside after the 2001 season.

Just when you thought legal troubles and a third suspension from the league would be the worst of Russell's worries, he died in an automobile accident in 2005 in Southern California.

If you don't think he deserves to be labeled a bust because of his early career prowess, that's probably fair.

But it's not as if the Raiders' other busts can match the tremendous disappointment Russell's career provided.

The next biggest busts are kicker Sebastian Janikowksi (Class of 2000) and offensive lineman Robert Gallery (2004). Both have had their ups and downs, and they've certainly had some fine moments, but not enough considering where they were drafted.

Janikowski was the 17th overall pick. That's just absurd, unless he's kicking game-winning field goals every week, which he isn't. Through eight seasons, Janikowski had no walk-off field goals. He thought he had one in Week Two at Denver in 2007, but Broncos coach Mike Shanahan called a timeout just before Janikowski's kick, and Janikowski missed his follow-up attempt. He made 13 of 21 field-goal attempts from at least 40 yards in 2007, surely not what you'd expect from a 17th overall pick.

Although Gallery fared quite well at left guard in 2007, left guards aren't number two picks. He was projected as a franchise left tackle when the Raiders took him second overall out of Iowa, and he's started at every spot on the line but center.

Among the other first-round busts: stone-handed tight end Rickey Dudley (ninth pick, 1996), offensive linemen Mo Collins (23rd, 1998) and Matt Stinchcomb (18th, 1999), safety Derrick Gibson (28th, 2001), and cornerback/returner Phillip Buchanon (17th, 2002). Cornerback Fabian Washington (23rd, 2005) also should be lumped into that group, having lost his starting job in 2007 and getting traded to Baltimore in 2008 for a fourth-round draft pick (wide receiver Arman Shields).

That's a pretty deep list of busts, but none compare to the disappointment from Darrell Russell's troubled career.

WHAT'S THE RAIDERS' BEST TRADE EVER?

Just when you thought the Raiders were done overhauling their roster in a busy March 2008, they went and pulled off a blockbuster trade, acquiring cornerback DeAngelo Hall from the Atlanta Falcons in exchange for a 2008 second-round draft pick and a 2009 fifth-round choice. Hall also got a whopper of a new contract that paid him $25 million guaranteed.

Could it evolve into the greatest trade in Raiders history? It faces some stiff competition.

Drift way back to 1967 and you'll see the Raiders came away with quite a bounty in the offseason, grabbing quarterback Daryle Lamonica, quarterback/kicker George Blanda, and cornerback Willie Brown via trades. (Side note: John Madden also arrived that year as the franchise's first linebackers coach.)

Lamonica served most of his first six seasons with the Raiders as their starter, leading the AFL in passing in 1969 and finishing with just over 19,000 yards by the time he retired after the 1974 season. Lamonica had 10 300-yard passing games—second in franchise history to Rich Gannon's 19—and he once threw six touchdown passes before halftime, that feat occurring in 1969 against Buffalo.

Yet another bountiful trade in 1967 brought Blanda to the Raiders. Used primarily as their kicker, Blanda became the Raiders' all-time scoring leader with 863 points. He was also a clutch quarterback when called upon, and he completed the second-longest pass in Raiders history, a 94-yard connection with Warren Wells in 1968 at Denver.

You know a trade is an oldie but a goodie when the Pro Football Hall of Fame displays the telegram announcing it. That's the case with the Raiders' 1967 deal for future Hall of Fame cornerback Willie Brown.

To nab Brown, as well as quarterback Mickey Slaughter, Al Davis sent the Denver Broncos defensive tackle Rex Mirich and a third-round draft pick. Brown played 12 of his 16 seasons with the Raiders, and "Old Man Willie" helped lock up their Super Bowl XI victory with a 75-yard interception return for a touchdown.

Brown shares the Raiders' all-time lead with 39 interceptions, and he's remained one of the most loyal Raiders. He's assisted Raiders coaching staffs for over 20 years and continues to tutor young defensive backs, such as should-be Pro Bowl pick Nnamdi Asomugha.

Brown and Blanda weren't the last Hall of Famers the Raiders acquired by trade. Others were offensive tackle Bob Brown (1971), cornerback Mike Haynes (1983), and James Lofton (1987), the latter two playing only for the Los Angeles Raiders, we should note. Linebacker Ted Hendricks arrived in 1975, with the Raiders shipping two

147

first-round picks to Green Bay in order to sign the future Hall of Famer.

Of all the trades, Willie Brown's arrival stands as the Raiders' best deal of all time. He came from a rival squad for a sweet price, and he delivered a Hall of Fame career. Over 40 years later, Al Davis has shown he isn't afraid to search for a better deal. So good luck with that, DeAngelo Hall. At least Brown is around to give Hall tips on how to make a trade super beneficial for the Silver and Black.

WHO WAS AL'S BEST COACHING HIRE?

The more the Raiders keep losing, the greater Jon Gruden's coach tenure (1998–2001) is looking.

Bringing in a 34-year-old Gruden from the Philadelphia Eagles was a nifty coup for Al Davis. Gruden inherited a 4–12 team, seized the reins hard, and after two 8–8 seasons, he ended the Raiders' six-year playoff drought by delivering postseasons with the 2000 and 2001 clubs, which went 12–4 and 10–6, respectively.

But Davis had a more daring coaching hire in 1969, promoting 32-year-old John Madden from linebackers coach to replace John Rauch.

Madden produced not only the Raiders' first Super Bowl title with the 1976 team, he produced what still ranks as the best winning percentage (.759, 103–32–7) among coaches with at least 100 victories. That earned him long overdue entry into the Pro Football Hall of Fame in 2006.

Forty years earlier, Madden was sitting on a bench outside of San Diego State's locker room and, as the Aztecs' defensive coordinator, he was formulating a game plan for a showdown with North Dakota State. Soon he was swapping strategies for an hour with Davis, who was in town scouting for the Raiders. In the offseason, Rauch interviewed Madden to become the Raiders' first linebackers coach, and when Rauch fled for the Buffalo Bills in 1969, Madden passed on a chance to follow him there, and instead bid on the Raiders head-coaching gig.

Despite being only 32, Madden made a convincing sales pitch to Davis, telling him he wouldn't be any better a coach in two years than he was then. The more Madden talked, the more Davis figured what the heck. Madden lasted 10 seasons, one more than Tom Flores, his successor and former assistant. Flores won two Super Bowls, so that's got to rate as a quality hire, too.

Madden is the best coach the Raiders have had, though. His shrewd game management, his boisterous style, and his successful record serve as the benchmark for the parade of coaches who've followed in his footsteps the past 30 years.

WHAT WAS AL'S WORST COACHING MOVE?

43 Consistency used to rule the Raiders' coaching ranks. Not so much anymore. Al Davis made four coaching changes between 2002–07, and none backfired more than the 2006 (re)hiring of Art Shell, who produced a league-worst 2–14 mark in his cameo that lasted just one season.

Shell was a sideline statue on game days. A pleasant man and a Hall of Fame guard, he failed miserably in his second stint as the Raiders coach. Remember New Coke? New Shell was worse. He lost his first five games, and his final nine. His team scored a league-low 10.5 points per game, a feat that was bound to happen when he chose an offensive coordinator (Tom Walsh) who had not coached in the NFL since 1994, when he got fired at the end of Shell's first reign as Raiders coach.

Shell's year-long feud with wide receiver Jerry Porter was a distraction, and an inability to spark Randy Moss looks even worse after Moss's record-setting 2007 with New England. Shell enjoyed much better days in his first stint as Raiders coach in Los Angeles, producing four winning seasons and three playoff berths in four-plus seasons from 1989–94.

But was Shell the worst coaching move by Davis? Jon Gruden did pretty dang well in his four seasons. That made his January 2002 exit quite painful for the Raiders Nation, which beloved the man they so often compared to the "Chucky" horror doll.

Not to get too deeeeeep and phil-o-soph-i-cal—as Gruden would say—but a still highly questionable move on Davis' part was him not paying Gruden a lucrative extension and instead trading him to the Tampa Bay Buccaneers in 2002. Gruden had led the Raiders out of the AFC West cellar and all the way to the AFC Championship Game, losing there to cap a 12–4 regular season in 2000.

But after a 10–4 campaign the next year that ended with the "Tuck Rule" playoff loss to the upstart New England Patriots, Gruden made a middle-of-the-night escape out of Oakland. All that was missing was a Baltimore Mayflower moving truck outside Gruden's Pleasanton home. The Tampa Bay Buccaneers traded for Gruden's services in exchange for two first-round draft picks, two second-round choices, and $8 million.

We're nearly 20 years past another classic coaching move by Davis, who canned Mike Shanahan four games into his second season as the Los Angeles Raiders' coach, and they've feuded ever since over Shanahan's alleged unpaid salary. Shell replaced Shanahan and posted only one losing season before getting fired after the 1994 campaign.

One of the cruelest moves of Davis' era came on Christmas Eve 1996, when he fired Mike White after two seasons as Raiders coach. Next up was Joe Bugel and a 4–12 season got him quickly canned.

After Lane Kiffin also posted a 4–12 in 2007 in his first year with the Raiders, he was coaching at the Senior Bowl when a bizarre report surfaced that Davis drew up Kiffin's resignation letter. Then again, nothing's quite bizarre anymore when it comes to Davis and his coaches.

Dire seasons call for Davis' countermeasures. Through the years, no move went sour more than Shell II, for not only was the franchise in further shambles, but Shell's image was hit hard, and that should never happen to a man whose bust resides in Canton.

WHICH EX-49ER BEST EXTENDED HIS CAREER WITH THE RAIDERS?

Ever since the Raiders opened for business in 1960, a pipeline of former 49ers players has flowed across the Bay to Oakland.

Four former 49ers helped lead the Raiders back to the Super Bowl in the 2002 season: wide receiver Jerry Rice, running back Charlie Garner, linebacker Bill Romanowski, and safety Rod Woodson.

We learned of Rice signing with the Raiders in 2001 thanks to an apparent slip of the tongue by Bill Walsh, the former 49ers coach who originally drafted Rice in 1985. The day Rice got released from the 49ers in June 2001, Walsh showed up at Rice's golf tournament in Los Altos and told the media: "I'm glad it's the Raiders. I'm glad it's close and that he doesn't feel he's being shipped to Devil's Island somewhere in the Midwest. I think he'll do very well over there."

Rice sure did do well, especially in that 2002 AFC-winning season. He totaled 92 catches for 1,211 yards and earned his 13th and final trip to the Pro Bowl. Rice played three-plus seasons for the Raiders before getting traded to Seattle during the 2004 season.

Running back Roger Craig and safety Ronnie Lott both left the 49ers for the Los Angeles Raiders in 1991 during Plan B free agency. Lott had a league-high eight interceptions in the first of his two seasons with the Raiders. Craig ran for just 590 yards and one touchdown in his lone season with the Raiders.

Other 49ers who evolved into Raiders include fullback Tom Rathman, center Jeremy Newberry, tight end Ted Kwalick, running back Terry Kirby, quarterback Rick Mirer, guard Ron Stone, defensive tackle Dana Stubblefield, tight end Earl Cooper, linebacker Riki Ellison, and defensive end Charlie Powell, one of the original Raiders in 1960.

But there's no greater success story among 49ers-turned-Raiders than quarterback Jim Plunkett's. Like many ex-49ers who traded sides of the Bay, Plunkett ended his career in the Silver and Black.

Plunkett's career very nearly was finished in 1978 when the 49ers cast him adrift after two seasons. But the number one overall draft pick by the New England Patriots in 1971 found new life with the Raiders. He quarterbacked them to their last two Super Bowl victories, starting with MVP honors in Super Bowl XV while completing a then-record 80-yard touchdown strike to Kenny King in that 27–10 win over Philadelphia in 1981. Former 49ers defensive end Cedrick Hardman was also part of that Raiders' Super Bowl-winning team.

WHICH OLD-TIME RAIDER IS MOST OVERDUE FOR THE HALL OF FAME?

If you ask Raiders patriarch Al Davis which former Raiders he'd like to join him next in the Pro Football Hall of Fame, you'll quickly hear not just one or two names, but many more. There's wide receiver Cliff Branch, punter Ray Guy, cornerback Lester Hayes, Coach Tom Flores, front-office wizard Ron Wolf, and quarterbacks Jim Plunkett, Ken Stabler, and Daryle Lamonica.

All are worthy candidates. But if you had to pick one, who do you go with?

Davis is aghast that Branch has been denied entry to the Hall of Fame, despite playing on all three of the Raiders' Super Bowl-winning teams and enjoying a productive 14-year career with the team. Branch was a four-time Pro Bowl pick and three-time All-Pro, and he averaged an outstanding 24.2 yards per catch in the 1976 season.

Two former Raiders whose names have repeatedly gone deep in the Hall of Fame selection process are Guy and Hayes. No other punter has been enshrined in Canton, but Guy figures to be the first if Hall voters are willing to open that door. Guy's leg routinely helped the

Raiders win the field-position battle, and he, like Branch, won three Super Bowls. As for Hayes, he was a five-time Pro Bowl player in his 10-year Raiders career, and no season went better than the 1980 Super Bowl campaign, when he totaled a league-high 13 interceptions in the regular season and five more in the postseason.

Flores deserves more consideration, if he's even gotten any at all by Hall voters. Not only did he win two Super Bowls—doing so with the 1980 and '83 Raiders—he became the first minority coach to secure a Lombardi Trophy. That feat has been widely overlooked, even in 2007, when the Indianapolis Colts' Tony Dungy and the Chicago Bears' Lovie Smith famously became the first black coaches to reach a Super Bowl.

The league has made a big push in recent years to increase minority hiring at the coaching and front-office levels. That should draw attention to Flores, who also became the first Hispanic to quarterback an American pro football team, doing so when he joined the Raiders in 1960. As a coach, Flores produced a winning team in six of nine seasons with the Raiders, and he was an assistant to Hall of Fame coach John Madden on the 1976 team that won Super Bowl XI.

Madden, by the way, hopes that safety Jack Tatum someday joins him in the Hall of Fame. Madden raves about Tatum's hard-nosed instincts and how great he was to coach. Unfortunately, Tatum's candidacy forever will be

157

overshadowed by his hit that paralyzed New England Patriots wide receiver Darryl Stingley in 1977.

Who else should we consider? Why quarterbacks, of course. And although Plunkett quarterbacked the Raiders to two Super Bowl titles, it's Stabler who has the edge when it comes to next Raider worthy of a Hall of Fame invitation. Stabler even made it among the 26 semifinalists for the 2008 Hall of Fame class.

A four-time Pro Bowl pick, Stabler led the league in touchdown passes (27) and passer rating (103.4) during the 1976 Raiders' run to the franchise's first Lombardi Trophy. His .661 winning percentage as a starter (96–49–1) ranks third behind only Joe Montana (.713) and Terry Bradshaw (.677), and just ahead of Steve Young (.657). That sounds Hall of Fame-esque in our book, so send The Snake to Canton.

SHOULD THE RAIDERS RETIRE "00"?

No one's allowed to wear No. 00 in the NFL anymore, not since the league's jersey-numbering system took root in 1973. So, in a way, Jim Otto's "00" is already immortalized.

But if the Raiders ever change their policy and retire a number for the first time, Otto's goose eggs deserve that honor. And Otto ought to get it. Now.

He's widely recognized as the ultimate Raider. He was one of the team's original players when the Raiders debuted in 1960, and he never missed a game in 15 seasons. He holds the franchise record with 210 consecutive starts, and he played in 308 games counting preseason, playoff, and All-Star games. He's also had 3,000 surgeries on his battered body. Okay, not 3,000, but over 50, including the amputation of his right leg in 2007.

Otto isn't one to downplay the importance of keeping "00" on the shelf. He strongly opposed center LeCharles Bentley's desire to wear "00" upon signing with the Cleveland Browns in 2006. Bentley unsuccessfully petitioned the NFL to bring "00" out of retirement so he could pay homage to Otto, his childhood idol.

Otto's response: "To let him wear my number, that I built into a legacy, all it takes is one ounce of coke up his nose and that legacy is gone," Otto told the *Contra Costa Times*. "I don't know who he is. I played 15 years with the Raiders. He's played, what, three or four years in New Orleans? What kind of legacy would he give double zero? I don't think he should wear it and I don't think anyone in the NFL should wear it."

Otto's the only Raider to have worn "00." The last NFL player to wear "00" was Houston Oilers wide receiver Kenny Burrough, who played from 1970–81 and was allowed to keep wearing those digits because he had 00 before it was outlawed by the 1973 jersey rules.

Other Raider greats, meanwhile, have had their numbers recycled over the years. Now, if the Raiders were willing to open the floodgates and start retiring jerseys, here are numbers that would merit consideration: 16 (George Blanda/Jim Plunkett), 22 (Mike Haynes), 24 (Willie Brown, not Charles Woodson or Michael Huff), 25 (Fred Biletnikoff), 32 (Marcus Allen), 63 (Gene Upshaw), 75 (Howie Long), 78 (Art Shell), 81 (Tim Brown), 83 (Ted Hendricks), and 87 (Dave Casper). But it all needs to start with Otto's 00. And if anyone objects, we suggest you take it up with Otto, who's rightfully proud of his number and could probably still pound you into submission.

WAS THE RAIDERS' TRADING OF RANDY MOSS THE NFL'S BIGGEST STEAL?

They traded Oakland for Los Angeles (and vice versa). They dealt Coach Jon Gruden to the Tampa Bay Buccaneers, and he promptly beat the Raiders in the Super Bowl. But when it comes to player trades, the Raiders' 2007 exportation of wide receiver Randy Moss might be viewed as the Raiders' worst of all time.

What we want to know, though, is whether the Patriots' made the biggest steal in NFL history.

Moss helped the Patriots to the league's first 16–0 record, he landed his sixth Pro Bowl berth, and he caught 23 touchdown passes to eclipse Jerry Rice's single-season record of 22 back in 1987's 12-game season.

That's a tremendous payoff for a Patriots club that acquired Moss by giving up only a fourth-round draft pick, which the Raiders used on defensive back John Bowie.

Moss may have saved his Hall of Fame candidacy with a near-picture-perfect season in New England, including a touchdown catch that nearly held up as the winner in Super Bowl XLII. But it's not as though Moss has several more years left in that brittle body of his. And that leads to why his trade to New England can't be viewed as the number one steal in NFL history.

So many other epic thefts featured players who were just starting out their Hall of Fame careers. They weren't trying to resurrect themselves after getting dealt. Look at Brett Favre, as Atlanta's loss was Green Bay's legendary gain. Or consider Hall of Fame quarterbacks John Elway and Steve Young. Elway wouldn't start his career in Baltimore, so he went on to lead the Denver Broncos to five Super Bowls. Young got shipped out of Tampa Bay and into the 49ers dynasty, where he played the final 13 seasons of his career.

You can even argue that the Raiders may have had one of the all-time steals by getting young cornerback Willie Brown from the Denver Broncos in 1967 for defensive tackle Rex Mirirch and a third-round pick.

Of course, when it comes to NFL trades, the biggest bounty of all was swiped by the Dallas Cowboys in 1989. That's when they sent Herschel Walker north to Minnesota in return for seven premium draft picks and five players, which they used to build their 1990s dynasty. Walker, in return, failed to rush for more than 825 yards in any of his three ensuing seasons.

Moss, simply put, failed in his two seasons with the Raiders. Getting rid of him was the wise thing to do for the 2007 Raiders, even though they promptly suffered through a fifth straight losing season. Injuries helped ruin what started as an impressive first season with the Raiders in

2005, but then Moss soured on the hapless team. He wouldn't go all out for passes, and he voiced his displeasure about the organization on his nationally syndicated radio show.

With his reputation savaged, Moss's career—and, quite possibly, his Hall of Fame bid—were resurrected in New England, land of the Patriots' dynasty. He went from a lousy team whose offense was run by a B&B owner (Tom Walsh, proprietor of an Idaho guest ranch) to a red-hot franchise that boasts a much different B&B (Coach Bill Belichick and quarterback Tom Brady).

In return, the Raiders acquired a fourth-round draft pick, which they used on Bowie, who hadn't played a snap for the Raiders by the time Moss had broken the Patriots' single-season record for touchdown receptions.

On the same day Moss broke that Patriots' single-season mark, Raiders boss Al Davis told longtime Minnesota columnist Sid Hartman that he regretted trading away Moss just to appease some of his coaches. Whatever. It appeased much of the Raiders fan base, even as painful as it may have been to see Moss succeed elsewhere. But Raider Nation can at least take comfort in knowing it's not our pick as the biggest steal in NFL history.

WARRIORS

WHO HAD THE BIGGER UPSET, THE 2007 OR 1975 WARRIORS?

 In our what-have-you-done-for-me-lately world, the Warriors' 2007 win over the top-seeded Dallas Mavericks often has been called the greatest upset in NBA playoff history. Go back to 1975, however, and you'll find stiff competition for that title.

It doesn't get any bigger than winning a championship, which the Warriors did in '75 by knocking off the favored Washington Bullets, and they did so with a stunning 4–0 sweep. This latest generation of Warriors fans probably remembers little of that '75 championship season, other than Rick Barry and Coach Al Attles being the beacons of it. We forget about Clifford Ray, Keith (later known as Jamaal) Wilkes, George Johnson, Derrick Dickey, Jeff Mullins, Butch Beard, and Charles Dudley.

Barry's retired jersey number is honored inside Oracle. He led the way to that '75 championship, including a 36-point effort in Game 2 and a 38-point outing in the Game 4 clincher in Washington. The series started there, and it was Paul Smith who scored 20 off the bench to key the Game 1 win, 101–95.

Then it was back to the Bay Area, or, specifically, San Francisco's Cow Palace, which was used for Games 2 and 3 because of a scheduling conflict with the Warriors' usual home at the Oakland Coliseum Arena. Yes, that place was already booked, showing just how unexpected it was for the Warriors to still be playing in late May.

The Warriors were written off by many before that '75 season when they traded longtime star Nate Thurmond for Ray. But Barry came through with a phenomenal season, was complemented by an unheralded group, and the Warriors overcame a 3–2 deficit against Chicago in the dramatic Western Conference Finals.

The Bullets entered the NBA Finals off a 60-win regular season and an Eastern Conference Finals battle with Boston. Plus, they had Elvin Hayes, Wes Unseld, and Phil Chenier on their side. But it's the Warriors who ended up with rings on their fingers.

The Warriors were 1–3 in the regular season against the Bullets, including a 24-point loss in January at Washington. In the NBA Finals, the Warriors won the four games by a combined 16 points, including one-point victories in Games 2 and 4.

A lonely yellow banner hangs from the Oracle Arena rafters to honor that 1975 title. Banners aren't made to signify a first-round playoff upset, no matter how invigorating, inspiring, and unlikely, as the 2007 squad's was. And upsetting the Mavericks in the playoffs really wasn't that crazy of a notion for the 2007 Warriors. After all, the Warriors won all three of their 2007 regular-season meetings and had won six of their past seven overall. Plus, the Warriors were hot, going 16–5 down the stretch and even 9–1 in their final regular-season games. Mix in the motivational factor of Coach Don Nelson sticking it to his last employer, Mavericks owner Mark Cuban, and that series was ripe for an upset.

Then again, the Mavericks became just the second team in NBA history to win 65 or more regular-season games and fail to win the championship. They stood alone in terms of being the first number-one seed to lose to a number-eight seed in a seven-game series.

But at least they weren't swept, like the Bullets in 1975.

WHAT'S THE WARRIORS' ALL-TIME STARTING FIVE?

When determining the Warriors' top five players since the franchise moved to the Bay Area in 1962, four choices are almost automatic—Rick Barry, Wilt Chamberlain, Nate Thurmond, and Chris Mullin. Things get tricky, however, in finding that fifth player and figuring out whether Baron Davis, Tim Hardaway, or Sleepy Floyd was the Warriors' top point guard.

Before we get into the point-guard battle—which really is the crux of this debate—we should defend our choices for our other fab four.

Barry is recognized as the Warriors' ultimate star, having led them to their only NBA championship in 1975. He averaged 25.6 points per game in the regular season, 31.7 in the playoffs. His career-best mark was 35.6 points per game in 1966–67, which ended with a six-game loss in the NBA Finals to the Philadelphia 76ers. After that season, he bailed to go play in the ABA with the Oakland Oaks, who eventually moved to Washington D.C. and then Virginia. Barry returned to the Warriors in 1972 and, although his career is synonymous with the technique of underhanded free throws, the Bay Area still remembers him for delivering a championship in 1975.

As for Chamberlain, we really don't need to give you his resume, do we? Okay, here's the short version on the 7-foot-1 "Stilt": He knew how to score. That was a tad bit evident with his 100-point game in 1962 against the New York Knicks (he'd probably score 200 against them these days). He averaged an astonishing 50.4 points per game in 1961–62, and 41.5 per game throughout his five-and–a-half-year tenure with the Warriors. Chamberlain accompanied the Warriors on their 1962 move to the Bay Area, and after leading the league in scoring those first two seasons by the Bay, he headed back to Philadelphia in a trade with the 76ers midway through the 1964–65 season.

Thurmond established himself as a Hall of Famer while suiting up with the Warriors for the first 11 years of his 14-year career. A seven-time All-Star, he averaged 15 points and 15 rebounds in his career, numbers that dipped once he was traded from the Warriors to the Chicago Bulls in 1974 for Clifford Ray, a 1975 first-round draft pick, and cash.

Mullin arguably was the best pure shooter in Warriors history, averaging 20.1 points per game while making 51.3 percent of his field-goal attempts in 13 seasons with them, which was capped by a 20-game stint in 2000–01 after a three-year layover in Indiana. Mullin joined the Warriors in 1985 out of St. John's, and the New Yorker with the crew cut quickly became a beloved figure among Bay Area sports fans. It didn't take long before he averaged over 25 points per game for five straight seasons, from 1988–89 to 1992–93. He helped key the Warriors' resurgence, just as he's done as their vice president of basketball operations, a role he assumed in 2004.

Okay, now let's finish out our starting five and pick a point guard.

While Hardaway's received more accolades than Davis or Floyd, Davis has emerged as one of the NBA's best point guards and he brought a desperately needed spark to the Warriors after arriving in a February 2005 trade. Had Davis not bailed for the Clippers in 2008 after three-plus seasons, he could have had a bigger impact and possibly been the winner in this debate.

Floyd played for the Warriors from 1982–87, and he's best remembered for his 51-point outburst in a 1987 playoff win over the Lakers, whom he really finished off with a 29-point fourth quarter in that Game 4 victory. Floyd averaged 17.7 points per game in his Warriors tenure, and we're looking for a little more production from our point guard, so let's scout out Hardaway's line. Okay, Hardaway averaged 19.8 points per game from 1989–96, but that average jumped to 25 during the 1991 and '92 playoffs.

Hardaway wasn't just a leg on the Run TMC scoring tripod with Mullin and Mitch Richmond. He popularized the "killer crossover" dribble that many of today's players use—or at least attempt to mimic. Hardaway collected

5,000 points and 2,500 assists faster than anyone other than Oscar Robertson.

Both Hardaway and Davis have enjoyed their finest offensive seasons in Don Nelson's fast-paced system with the Warriors. Both were determined leaders, clutch shooters, and confident floor generals.

Both averaged about 20 points per game in the regular season, 25 points per game in the playoffs. In two post-seasons for the Warriors, Hardaway averaged 25 points, 10 assists, 3.2 steals, and 3.7 rebounds per game over 13 games. Davis averaged 25.3 points, 6.5 assists, 2.9 steals, and 4.5 rebounds per game in the 2007 Playoffs.

Hardaway was 52 games into his sixth season with the Warriors when he got traded to the Miami Heat, arriving in time to partake in the first of six straight playoff appearances there.

He also gained the league-wide respect that's eluded Davis, who truly deserves more recognition for all he did in his short time in O-town. Hardaway made three straight All-Star Games from 1991–93. Davis didn't make the All-Star Game in his first three full seasons with the Warriors, and, he didn't make our Warriors all-time starting unit, with the final spot going to Hardaway.

WHAT COACHING ERA WAS BETTER, NELLIE I OR NELLIE II?

50 From the day Don Nelson returned for his second stint as Warriors coach, you could tell that this era was going to be different, and better than his first one. Nelson walked into the locker room that first day back in 2006 and informed his players of The 66 Rule, as defined by, "I'm 66 and I don't give a (hoot)."

Oh, he cared plenty about ending the Warriors' 12-year playoff drought. He just didn't care about any complaints, egos, checkered pasts, draft statuses, or other bad karma those Warriors possessed.

The 2006–07 Warriors not only finished as the NBA's second-highest scoring team, they captivated the nation with a riveting playoff run that included a sensational first-round upset of the top-seeded Dallas Mavericks, who had won 67 of 82 regular-season games. That team made the Bay Area fall in love with basketball again.

Nellie's first stint as Warriors coach (1988–95) also produced a playoff-series victory in his first season, as the W's swept Utah before being eliminated by Phoenix. His teams reached the postseason in three more seasons.

Nellie's initial stint as Warriors coached ended in February 1995, following a contentious start to the season and the devastating trade of Chris Webber.

So what makes Nellie II better than Nellie I? Nellie II features a more matured coach who'd been through hard knocks in stops with the New York Knicks and Dallas Mavericks. He had instant respect when he walked back into the Warriors locker room in 2006, doing so after spending the previous season in his Maui abode. He developed a wonderful kinship with point guard Baron Davis, who didn't get along with his previous two coaches. And Nellie showed his more matured side when he stunningly welcomed Webber back to the Warriors in January 2008, a reunion that stalled out of the gate and quickly led to Webber's retirement.

Nellie is the second-winningest coach in NBA history, and his fast-paced, helter-skelter style is unique and entertaining. He's also a media favorite, giving colorful quotes filled with candor. No coach in the Bay Area can match his forthright approach.

In Nellie II, he hasn't hesitated to criticize his players (The 66 Rule!) or downplay his team's chances to contend for a championship. Some dismissed that as simple motivational techniques, like when he declared the 2006–07 seasons playoff hopes dead on February. 28. The Warriors went 16–5 down the stretch, including a 9–1 mark at the very end of the regular season to reach the playoffs.

In between Nellie's two stints, the Warriors burned through eight coaches—Bob Lanier, Rick Adelman, P.J. Carlesimo, Garry St. Jean, Dave Cowens, Brian Winters, Eric Musselman, Mike Montgomery—and not one produced a winning team.

As exciting as Nellie II has been, it likely won't last as long as Nellie's first term that went six and a half seasons. It took great convincing (see: pay raise) to convince him to return for 2007–08, and it's doubtful he'll be around to institute The 70 Rule, as defined by, "I'm 70 and I really, really don't give a (hoot)."

WAS "THE DUNK" REALLY THE WARRIORS' BEST?

Baron Davis emphatically put an exclamation mark on the Warriors' 2007 playoff run with what immediately became known as "The Dunk." It was a phenomenal slam in front of a hysterical home crowd, and that atmosphere will give it an infinite shelf life in Warriors lore.

Perhaps, someday, Nike will even do a commercial about it, as one was done in 1994 off Chris Webber's behind-the-back dunk over Charles Barkley.

There's no shortage of video replays of The Dunk, and it even led off the pregame festivities at 2007–08 home games, with a Jumbotron subtitle of "Where amazing happens."

Why was it so amazing? Davis poster-ized Utah's Andrei Kirilenko. Davis blew past Jazz point guard Deron Williams, elevated along the left baseline with his rickety knees, slammed his left forearm into Kirilenko's face, and then hammered the ball through the rim with his right hand.

The Warriors already had a 20-point lead with three minutes to go in Game 3 of their Western Conference Semifinal when Davis capped off his 34-point showing with

The Dunk. The crowd erupted. The awed Warriors bench had priceless reactions. And Davis relished the moment, lifting up his jersey to reveal a blue girdle (or an abdominal supporter), and thus drawing a technical foul.

Kirilenko accepted his place in Warriors lore, noting in the postgame press conference that, "at least I got on the poster." No word yet if Kirilenko is getting any royalties from possible poster sales.

Davis said he shocked himself with The Dunk. But there would be no more surprises from the Warriors, whose playoff run came to an end by losing the next two games against the Jazz.

Did The Dunk inspire the Jazz? Well, the way the Warriors failed to match up with Utah's bruisers, that series wasn't going to go Golden State's way, anyhow. So embrace The Dunk.

Now, if you're looking for The Other Dunk by a Warrior, how about the one Webber threw down in his 1993–94 rookie season?

Webber took an outlet pass from Latrell Sprewell and looped the ball around his back en route to a breakaway jam over the Suns' Barkley. When the Warriors and Suns met in the postseason, Webber's dunk became the subject of a Nike commercial, in which he and Sprewell recreate it in a barbershop.

Like Davis' Dunk, Webber's also may have backfired and led to a postseason ouster. The Suns completed a three-game, first-round sweep of the Warriors when Barkley put up 56 points in the Game 3 finale.

Other memorable dunks in the Warriors archives include Jason Richardson's dunk-contest winners, Latrell Sprewell's two-handed jams, and Phil Smith's slam against Elvin Hayes in the 1975 Finals. But The Dunk set a new standard, at least for the Warriors.

It's not Dr. J rocking the cradle in 1983 for the 76ers. It's not John Starks blowing up the Bulls in 1993. It's not Darryl Dawkins breaking glass in '79, or Shaquille O'Neal bringing down the whole basket stand in '93. It's not a Dominique Wilkins windmill or a Spud Webb dunk-contest thriller. And Air Baron won't be mistaken for Air Jordan.

But The Dunk, until further notice, stands as THE Dunk by a Warrior.

WHO'S THE WARRIORS' BIGGEST DRAFT BUST?

The Warriors are experts at finding first-round flops. So who's the top flopper?

One contender is certainly Joe Smith. In 1995, the Warriors took the forward who's had a long and serviceable career. Just not for the Warriors. Smith lasted two and a half seasons in Golden State. What's worse—the next four draft picks after Smith were Antonio McDyess, Jerry Stackhouse, Rasheed Wallace, and high schooler Kevin Garnett. Ouch.

The Warriors' path to the number one pick in 1980 was more infamous than the guy they actually drafted, Joe Barry Carroll. To acquire the numbers one and 13 picks, the Warriors dealt Robert Parrish and the number three overall pick, which the Boston Celtics used on Kevin McHale. Carroll got shipped out (to Houston) in his seventh season, by which time the Celtics were en route to their fifth NBA Finals since 1980.

When talking busts, you really can't go wrong mentioning Todd Fuller, the number 11 pick in 1996 who was drafted ahead of Kobe Bryant (13th), Peja Stojakovic (14th), and Steve Nash (15th). Fuller started 18 games as a rookie, then just once in 57 games the following season.

The Warriors traded him in February 1999 to Utah for a second-round draft pick.

In 1997, the year after picking Fuller, the Warriors blew a top-10 pick on center Adonal Foyle, who was so much better off the court than on it, and he's got the community service awards to prove it. Foyle went eighth overall, and Toronto nabbed Tracy McGrady ninth.

Not to be forgotten in bust talk is the sad case of Cyril Baptiste. His career was ruined by drugs, and Baptiste never played in a regular-season game. He was a 1971 supplemental draft pick and, with that selection, the Warriors forfeited their 1972 first-round draft pick.

Mike Dunleavy's selection with the number three pick in 2002 will stir some bust talk and for good reason. But he's certainly not the worst, and at least the Warriors got some value out of him, trading him to Indianapolis in an eight-player deal that sparked the Warriors' 2007 playoff run.

No, the worst is Chris Washburn, the number three overall draft pick in 1986.

Drug problems derailed Washburn's career from the outset, and three years after the Warriors drafted him, he got banned for life from the NBA for drug abuse.

Washburn played only 35 games as a rookie, taking a sidetrip to drug rehab in January 1987. He played eight games the next season before then-GM Don Nelson got the Atlanta Hawks to trade for him. In return, the Warriors got the rights to Ken Barlow, a European league player who never did suit up for the Warriors. Nelson didn't mind that, so long as Washburn was no longer the Warriors' problem.

While more problems seemingly surface with every draft—or disappointing position in the draft lottery—the Warriors will have a hard time delivering a worse draft pick than Washburn. Keep his troubled career in mind when you start frowning upon the scant production from recent first-round picks, including Patrick O'Bryant (number nine overall, 2006), and Marco Belinelli (number 18, 2007). If the Warriors continue to discover more second-round gems like Monta Ellis (2005) and Gilbert Arenas (2001), maybe, just maybe, it'll be a lot easier to forget about Washburn and other draft busts. Then again, maybe not.

BETTER 51-POINT OUTBURST: SLEEPY OR JAMISON?

53 The best scoring exhibition in Warriors history is, of course, the greatest in NBA history—Wilt Chamberlain's 100-point game. But that was for the Philadelphia Warriors in 1962. When it comes to more recent outbursts by a Golden State Warrior, we have two prime contenders: Sleepy Floyd's 51-point show in the 1987 playoffs and Antawn Jamison's back-to-back 51-point games in 2000.

What made Floyd's game so legendary, of course, were the 29 points he scored in the fourth quarter of that May 10, 1987, win over the Los Angeles Lakers. He missed his first shot of the fourth quarter, then made 12 consecutive field goals, along with five free throws, for an unforgettable Game 4 win in the Western Conference Semifinal.

That 129–121 victory saved the Warriors from being eliminated (which they were anyhow, however in Game 5, 118–106.)

Floyd's NBA playoff-record 29-point spree featured mostly driving layups capped by finger rolls or a scoop shot. No one-trick pony, though, as he also had an off-balance bank shot in there and a jumper near the free throw line. Not to be forgotten is who he did this against, the eventual NBA-champion Lakers, the "Showtime" unit of Magic Johnson, Kareem Abdul-Jabbar, James Worthy, Michael Cooper, Byron Scott, and A.C. Green.

On December 6, 2000, Jamison's 51 led the Warriors to a 125–122 overtime win at Oakland against, get this, the Lakers. Three days earlier, Jamison also scored 51 in a three-point loss in Seattle.

Jamison's encore effort was additionally amazing because of the scoring duel that ensued between him and Kobe Bryant, who also scored 51 points. Jamison had eight points in overtime and finished 21 of 29 from the field.

Four decades earlier, Chamberlain (63 points) and Elgin Baylor (51) had their own scoring duel in a Warriors-Lakers matchup. The Warriors have had higher-scoring games from others besides Chamberlain, Floyd, and Jamison. Rick Barry scored 64 against Portland in '74, and his 55-point effort against the 76ers in 1967 still stands as a Warriors playoff record. Purvis Short also broke the 50-point barrier twice in 1984.

But in terms of sheer drama, nothing still resonates in the memory of Warriors fans like Floyd's 51-point game, or, specifically, his 29-point fourth quarter. Considering Floyd's circumstances (huge fourth quarter in an elimination game), Jamison couldn't trump Floyd with his own 51-point showing, even if it was his second straight game with 51.

54 The Warriors' recent revival—after 12 dormant years out of the playoffs—came in large part to two terrific trades swung by Chris Mullin, a former star guard-turned-personnel executive. They landed point guard Baron Davis in Februrary 2005, then two years later, Stephen Jackson and Al Harrington arrived in an eight-player deal with the Indiana Pacers.

Davis has thrived under Coach Don Nelson, hitting some absurd clutch shots and bringing certified star power to the franchise. Jackson's defense, leadership, and fearless shooting has been a perfect complement to Davis, and Harrington has had some nice moments as a part-time starter or quality sixth man.

Unfortunately for the Warriors, not all their trades worked out as well as those two.

No trade may have stung as quickly as the January 1965 exportation of Wilt Chamberlain to the 76ers, in exchange for Connie Dierking, Paul Neumann, Lee Shaffer, and cash. The following season, Chamberlain's 76ers beat the Warriors 4–2 in the NBA Finals.

No trade sent the Warriors reeling as badly as the 1994 deal in which they bid farewell to Rookie of the Year Chris

Webber. A 50-win team with Webber in 1993–94, the Warriors went 26–56 without him the next year, and so began their stretch of 12 seasons without a playoff appearance.

But no Warriors trade was more lopsided than the one on June 9, 1980, the eve of that year's draft. It's a date that lives in infamy for Bay Area fans and a date Boston fans should forever celebrate.

It's when the Warriors dealt center Robert Parrish and the number three pick in the 1980 draft to the Celtics, who used that pick on forward Kevin McHale to complete the NBA's best-ever front line with Larry Bird. What did the Warriors get? They moved up two spots in the draft to take center Joe Barry Carroll, and they also received the number 13 choice, used on guard Rickey Brown, who averaged 5.2 points in two-plus seasons.

Carroll wasn't a spectacular bust—he made the 1987 All-Star Game—but his six and a half seasons with the Warriors featured only one playoff appearance. He averaged 20.4 points per game, and his Warriors tenure was interrupted by a one-year stint abroad in the Italian league.

As for the Celtics, they were headed for their fifth NBA Finals since 1980 when the Warriors unloaded Carroll in 1987 (along with Sleepy Floyd in exchange for Ralph Sampson and Steve Harris, who "helped" the Warriors to a 20–62 mark in 1987–88). Parrish, a 1976 Warriors draft pick, led the league in rebounds and blocks his first three years in Boston as he indeed went, as he put it, "from the outhouse to the penthouse."

185

WHY DON'T MORE PLAYERS SHOOT FREE THROWS UNDERHANDED?

 Warriors legend Rick Barry is the second-most accurate free throw shooter in NBA history, having gained that prestige with a unique underhand style. So why don't more NBA players go the granny route?

Because, in the words of tennis great Andre Agassi, image is everything.

Most of these guys are multimillionaires, so why sacrifice pride for a better free-throw percentage, huh? Well, Barry is one of the most prideful guys the NBA has ever known, yet he still can't convince others to follow his underhand lead, not even his four sons who've also gone on to pro careers—Jon, Brent, Drew, and Scooter.

Shaquille O'Neal has repeatedly rejected Barry's overtures to school him on the underhand free throw. O'Neal once claimed he'd shoot negative 30 percent before he shoots underhand. Well, let's say he's staying just above that watershed mark, as his career average is just over 50 percent on free throws.

Wilt Chamberlain, who left the Warriors a year before Barry's arrival in 1965, wrote in his autobiography that he "felt silly like a sissy" when he tried going underhand to solve his free throw epidemic.

Barry learned the craft from his father and among those he successfully passed it on to was George Johnson, a teammate on the Warriors' 1975 championship team. Barry was inducted into the Naismith Memorial Basketball Hall of Fame in 1987, 10 years after he concluded his Warriors career. His final two NBA seasons came with Houston, and he saved his best free throw shooting for last in those two seasons (160 of 169 in 1978–79, 143 of 153 in 1979–80).

While Barry remains the authority on free throw shooting, he's not the only one offering advice. Many NBA teams have hired shooting coaches to improve their showing at the charity stripe. Instructional videos are everywhere. Yet, so are clanked free throws.

Many theories abound why free throw shooting isn't as precise as it should be (and possibly could be if shooters went with the underhanded approach).

The Warriors brought in Sydney Moncrief to tutor their players on free throw shooting during the 2007–08 season. Now, if they'd only brought in Barry, maybe we'd actually see some underhanded attempts.

Warriors center Andris Biedrins has battled free throw woes in his career, but he's gone from a 30-percent shooter in 2005–06 to over 60 percent in 2007–08. He's improved after switching to a one-hand release in 2006. Biedrins said if he ever resorted to an underhand approach, then the next thing you know he might try to kick the ball, too.

Oh well, maybe that'll keep Barry's 90-percent free throw percentage safe atop the all-time list. Okay, it's not at the very top. That spot is held by Mark Price, who shot 90.4 percent in a four-year career that included a stint with …you guessed it, the Warriors, from 1996–97.

DID THE WARRIORS MAKE THE BEST APOLOGY IN SPORTS HISTORY?

As the Warriors wrapped up their 12th consecutive season without a playoff berth, a unique ad appeared in the Bay Area's newspapers on April 17, 2006. It was an apology, signed by all 14 players.

"Regrettably, we just didn't get it done for you," read the full-page ad. "We are committed to doing whatever it takes this summer to make the 2006–07 season one that you can be proud of."

The Warriors lived up to their word, pulling off a 42–40 season in 2006–07 that ended with one of the NBA's most exciting playoff runs in recent memory. Who gets the credit for the ad? Give it to Jason Richardson who got traded away after the 2006–07 season.

Richardson and team president Robert Rowell wanted to thank fans for setting a season attendance record despite the disappointing, 34–48 record. Richardson and the team split the cost of the $100,000 ad.

What's more amazing, an athlete spending his own coin for a team-wide apology or athletes actually fulfilling their vows for an improved season?

Another newspaper apology worth comparing was a full-page ad that New York Giants owner Horace Stoneham took out in Minneapolis newspapers in 1951. He did so to apologize to fans of the Triple-A Millers after calling up hot-hitting centerfielder Willie Mays, thus robbing Minnesota fans of further enjoying Mays' brilliance.

In contrast, think back to the apology Ryan Leaf read in the San Diego Chargers' locker room years ago. After shouting at a reporter, Leaf returned to the locker room to give that apology, and after reading it in a prepared statement, he promptly tossed that paper with disdain into his locker.

Another epic apology came when Terrell Owens, after being banished by the Philadelphia Eagles in 2005, read from a statement he admitted he didn't even write.

If the Richardson-led apology of 2006 was the Warriors' greatest, Latrell Sprewell's might be the worst. After getting into a December 1, 1997, altercation with Coach P.J. Carlesimo in practice and subsequently getting suspended, Sprewell told the New York Post a month later: "I'm not as bad as everyone has made me out to be. It's as if I'm another O.J. Simpson. Yes, I was wrong, but I didn't kill anybody. I'm not a double murderer."

Sprewell, by the way, was on the last Warriors team (1993–94) to reach the playoffs before the 2006–07 team ended that drought, doing so on the heels of one very public apology in newsprint.

GIANTS

DID BARRY BONDS KNOWINGLY USE PERFORMANCE-ENHANCING DRUGS?

Barry Bonds says he didn't. The government says he did. That debate spilled into San Francisco's Federal Building in 2007, a result of Bonds' November 15 indictment on four counts of perjury and one count of obstruction of justice regarding his 2003 grand jury testimony about never taking illegal performance-enhancing drugs.

In the court of public opinion, Bonds has already been convicted as a cheat, implying that he knew exactly what he was doing in an effort to become baseball's all-time best slugger.

Here's how the debate goes at your local bar:

Questioner: "Is Bonds guilty?"

Responder: "Hah! Does he bat left-handed?"

Questioner: "Yeah."

Responder: "See, it's a no-brainer."

The initial federal indictment cited 19 instances in which Bonds allegedly lied under oath during the government's investigation into the BALCO scandal, which stemmed from a 2003 federal raid on a Bay Area laboratory that also operated as a steroid ring. Much of Bonds' December 4, 2003, testimony had already been leaked three years earlier to the San Francisco Chronicle, so the government's allegations didn't come as a total shock.

Unless, of course, you bought what Bonds was selling on the 2007 summer night he broke Hank Aaron's home-run record. Bonds claimed on that August 7 evening: "This record is not tainted. At all. Period."

The debate undertaken by the government doesn't center on the record as much as whether Bonds told the truth in his 2003 sworn testimony. Prosecutors had granted Bonds immunity regarding any potential drug use, as long as he was truthful. They don't think he was. The overall public opinion agrees.

The government's indictment cited a November 2000 drug test in which a "Barry B." tested positive for two anabolic steroids. That apparent test was conducted independently as such tests weren't mandated by the league back in those stat-happy days. Bonds repeatedly testified that he did not take steroids or human-growth hormone and had never seen that positive test.

Bonds also testified that his personal trainer, Greg Anderson, rubbed some "cream" arthritis balm on his arm and gave him "flaxseed oil," later determined to be the "clear" designer steroid. And you thought Rice-A-Roni was the San Francisco treat, huh?

While those admissions of receiving the "cream" and "clear" might confirm your suspicions that Bonds used illegal methods to break baseball's home-run record, the government apparently based its case on much more. There reportedly are doping calendars, payment documents, and damning testimony from others who accuse Bonds of indeed knowing what he was doing. Kimberly Bell, Bonds' former girlfriend, reportedly testified that Bonds dove hard into performance-enhancing drugs once Mark McGwire stole the national spotlight with his 1998 home-run binge.

Now Bonds can't escape the spotlight, like when droves of media surrounded San Francisco's Federal Building on December 7, 2007, at which point he entered a not-guilty plea regarding the feds' indictment.

So did he or didn't he? The evidence—including Bonds' physical appearance and home-run prowess—are enough to convince us that he intentionally bulked up on steroids. Now the follow-up question is whether anyone really cares, outside of stat worshipers and baseball purists. He was a showman, a superstar slugger who demanded your attention for every one of his at-bats. Outside the federal building on that December day, Giants fans showed their support for the troubled slugger by wearing his jersey or shouting words of encouragement. Steroids or not, they loved watching him belt homers into McCovey Cove, and for that, there's no debate.

IS BONDS A FIRST-BALLOT HALL OF FAMER?

Barry Bonds' biggest defenders, as well as some impartial observers, will argue that he had Hall of Fame credentials even before a cloud of steroid-related suspicion arose at the turn of the millennium.

That said, Bonds likely won't be making it into Cooperstown in his first year of eligibility, especially if Mark McGwire's voting results are any indication. McGwire received less than 25 percent of the vote in his first two years of Hall of Fame eligibility, in 2007 and '08. Still fresh in voters' minds was McGwire's embarrassing refusal to talk about the past in his 2005 Congressional testimony.

Does Bonds deserve to be in the Hall of Fame? Absolutely. Will he be a first-ballot entrant? The Magic 8 Ball says: "Outlook not so good." Will he eventually make the Hall of Fame? Most likely, but it's a good bet that it won't happen in his first year of eligibility.

A "first-ballot" designation is reserved for not just the game's all-time legends, but also those who don't bring with them baggage that's severely stained the sport.

Do first-ballot Hall of Famers stand before a federal judge and plead not guilty to five felony charges? Are they despised by many of their peers for reasons other than clobbering them during games?

Still, Bonds did merit and receive respect from many, especially because his numbers—pre-2000 and post-2003—are Cooperstown-esque. He was among the best players in the game before the steroids era, and he was among the best after it, if there's really even been an end point.

Nevertheless, Bonds started every All-Star Game between 1992–98 and won Gold Gloves from 1990–98. At the plate, he delivered a potent presence, before and after his alleged steroid spree. On the basepaths, he was a tremendous threat, at least for the first half of his career, before he began focusing on home runs and drawing an endless number of walks.

Upon his heralded arrival with the Giants in 1993, he promptly won his third of seven National League MVP awards. Those final four MVP honors came in rapid-fire succession, from 2001–04, when the steroid era was in full swing.

Before leading the 2002 Giants to the World Series, Bonds had the most statistically awing season ever in baseball. That 2001 show featured 73 home runs (breaking McGwire's 1998 record) and a .863 slugging percentage (passing Babe Ruth's mark of .849).

By the time the Giants' booted Bonds out after the 2007 season, he ranked first all-time in home runs (762), second in RBIs (2,213, or 84 behind Hank Aaron), third in walks

(2,227, or 68 behind leader Rickey Henderson), and fifth in slugging percentage (.607; Ruth is first at .690). That's Hall of Fame stuff. And while Bonds demanded that the Hall turn away his 756th home-run ball if it's marked with an asterisk, he should be welcomed into Cooperstown so long as it's not a first-ballot selection. Consider that an asterisk on to his unparalleled career.

WHO ARE THE ALL-TIME BEST SAN FRANCISCO GIANTS?

Some made it to the World Series. Some won MVPs. Many were All-Stars. As Giants executive Larry Baer said at a February 2008 luncheon commemorating the team's 50th season in San Francisco, the biggest part about their history is the players. Without further adieu, here are the top ones at each position:

CATCHER: BOB BRENLY

Brenly emerged as a charismatic leader during the Giants' 1980s transition from cellar dweller to pennant contender. He statistically peaked in the 96-loss 1984 season, totaling 20 homers, 80 RBIs, a .291 batting average, and a hometown hero trip to the All-Star Game at Candlestick. Brenly earned the prestigous Willie Mac Award for his leadership in that 1984 season. He had one of baseball's best goat-to-hero moments ever on September 14, 1986, when he committed four errors at third base in the fourth inning but then hit the game-winning homer in the ninth with two outs and the count full.

Brenly's leadership helped key the 1987 team that delivered San Francisco its first National League West title since 1971. His outgoing personality has served him well in his post-playing career, whether it be working as a broadcaster or manager, or do we really have to remind you that he won a World Series in his first season as the Arizona Diamondbacks skipper in 2001? Here's some easier trivia to digest: Brenly is the only catcher to lead San Francisco in homers in a season, tallying just 19 in 1985 on that 100-loss team.

ON THE BENCH: Tom Haller, Dick Dietz, and Benito Santiago all make strong challengers to Brenly as the Giants' top catcher. Haller caught the most games in franchise history and was an All-Star his final two seasons, in 1966 and '67. Haller also had one of the Giants' five home runs in the 1962 World Series. Dietz had a phenomenal 1970 season (.300 batting average, 22 homers, 107 RBIs, All-Star) and fared well in the 1971 run to the NL West crown. Santiago recharged his career in San Francisco from 2001–03, highlighted by his 2002 NLCS MVP award but tainted by his connection to the BALCO steroids scandal.

FIRST BASE: WILLIE MCCOVEY

It's not a "Stretch" to pick the Hall of Famer with that nickname as the Giants' top first baseman, although this position has featured more marquee talent than any other in Giants lore. McCovey broke in with the Giants in 1959, going 4-for-4 with two triples in his debut—the self-proclaimed highlight of his career—en route to Rookie of the Year honors. Ten years later, he was the National League's MVP, belting a career-best 45 home runs. Willie Mac's first stint with the Giants lasted from 1959–73, and he won the Comeback Player of the Year award upon returning in 1977. Just before retiring in 1980, he delivered one final moment to cherish: A ninth-inning, pinch-hit double that lifted the Giants past the Dodgers on June 29, 1980.

He was so much more than just a slugger and consistent offensive threat (he had 22- and 24-game hit streaks early in his career). He played a swift first base, and he's so revered that the Giants annually give the Willie Mac Award to the most exemplary leader, an award Barry Bonds never won. McCovey was a six-time All-Star, and he hit two home runs en route to their 1969 Midsummer Classic's MVP honor.

ON THE BENCH: Hall of Famer Orlando Cepeda is first off the bench here. He had a memorable debut, too, homering in the Giants' first game in San Francisco in 1958. Cepeda won Rookie of the Year honors, went on to six All-Star Games, and still ranks high among the Giants' all-time offensive leaders. He departed in the worst Giants' trade ever, getting dealt to the St. Louis Cardinals for Ray Sadecki on May 8, 1966.

If there was a Hall of Fame for fan favorites, Will Clark and J.T. Snow belong in it. Clark's swagger and picturesque swing sparked the Giants' mid-1980s resurgence, capped with his clutch hitting in the 1989 NLCS victory. Snow's sensational glove work (franchise-best .966 career fielding percentage at first base) was always a thing of beauty.

SECOND BASE: JEFF KENT

Baseball had never seen a second baseman pack as much offensive punch as Kent did in his six full seasons with the Giants, from 1997 to the 2002 World Series run. A Cal product and constant sourpuss, Kent joined the Giants in a then-controversial trade for Matt Williams. Kent surprisingly became a superb complement to Barry Bonds in the lineup. He won National League MVP honors in 2000 with 33 homers and 125 RBIs, and he put up 37 homers and 108 RBIs in 2002 before fleeing in free agency to the Astros and then the dreaded Dodgers. That last season with the Giants ended in a World Series appearance, but the path there wasn't smooth. His spring featured a broken wrist that he tried blaming on a truck-washing accident rather than a motorcycle crash. He also got into a June fracas with Bonds in a San Diego dugout. But give Kent bonus points for standing up to Bonds. And give him some respect for his monster seasons with the Giants before converting to the dark side (the Dodgers).

ON THE BENCH: Robby Thompson became a quick fan favorite and embodied the team's 1986 slogan: "You Gotta

Like These Kids." A two-time All-Star, Thompson played his entire 11-year career with the Giants. Overshadowed by Will Clark upon their major-league debuts in 1986, Thompson still won the Sporting News' Rookie of the Year Award. Thompson's best season was 1993, the same year that featured an epic moment in Giants history: They were down to their last strike when he belted a two-run, walk-off homer for a 7–6 win over the Florida Marlins on August 22.

Another option at second base is Joe Morgan, who wound down his Hall of Fame career with the Giants in 1981 and '82. Morgan left the Giants with the perfect bang—a game-winning homer in the regular-season finale to keep the Dodgers out of the playoffs. Tito Fuentes (1965–74) is another respected second baseman locked into the Giants' archives, and he's still sticking around as a sentimental link to the team's past.

THIRD BASE: MATT WILLIAMS

Every bit the fielder, Williams was three times the hitter, and his production at the hot corner hasn't been matched since he left after the 1996 season. A first-round draft pick in 1986, Williams hit the majors in 1987 and enjoyed a 10-year stay with the Giants.

He won a classic 12-pitch duel in Game 4 of the 1989 NLCS against the Cubs, blasting a two-run homer off Steve Wilson in the Giants' 6–4 win. The 1994 strike spoiled

Williams's run at Roger Maris' single-season home run record, with his 34th home run coming August 10 in the abrupt season finale. Williams was runner-up in 1994 MVP voting, and he ranks fifth in the Giants' record book with 247 homers. Combining all that with his three Gold Gloves and love of the game, Williams's exportation to the Indians had Giants fans in despair, at least until Jeff Kent emerged as a sturdy offensive replacement.

ON THE BENCH: Jim Davenport's defense was exquisite, starting right away with his rookie season in the Giants' first year in San Francisco. A .258 lifetime hitter, he leads all Giants third basemen with a .964 fielding percentage in 1,130 games. Davenport garnered a Gold Glove and an All-Star spot during the Giants' 1962 path to the World Series. He also set a major-league record among third baseman with no errors in 97 consecutive games in 1966.

SHORTSTOP: RICH AURILIA

As steady as three-time All-Star Chris Speier was in the 1970s, Aurilia turned in offensive seasons rarely before seen by major league shortstops during his initial stint with the Giants (1995–2003). Cue the Beastie Boys' track "No Sleep 'Till Brooklyn," watch Aurilia settle into the batter's box, and give thanks he's no Johnnie LeMaster (.222 lifetime hitter).

Aurilia's maturity as a hitter really showed in his 2001 All-Star season, when he had 37 homers, 97 RBIs, a .324

batting average, and 206 hits, the second most in San Francisco Giants history behind Willie Mays' 208 in '58. Those 37 home runs put Aurilia in an exclusive club with Ernie Banks and Barry Larkin as the only National League shortstops with 30-homer seasons. That 2001 campaign actually marked Aurilia's third straight season with over 20 home runs.

Of course, it helped that he hit ahead of Bonds. But Aurilia, who returned to the Giants in 2007, was also a calming voice in the clubhouse during the circus that accompanied Bonds' road to the home-run record.

ON THE BENCH: Speier also had two tours of duty in his Giants career, splashing onto the scene with a stellar rookie season for the 1971 National League West winners. He was an All-Star the following three years, and made only 12 errors in 1975. Any debate about the Giants all-time shortstops would be incomplete without mentioning the popular Jose "Ooooo-Ree-Bay" Uribe, defensive maestro Omar Vizquel, and Jose Pagan, shortstop for the 1962 National League champs. Vizquel played 16 seasons in the American League (with the Mariners and Indians) before joining the Giants in 2005, winning a Gold Glove that year and in 2006.

LEFT FIELD: BARRY BONDS

From homering in his first home at-bat as a Giant in 1993, to covertly fleeing AT&T Park during the ninth inning of the Giants' 2007 home finale, Bonds put in 15 years of incredible service, no matter how controversial it was. The Bay Area's prodigal slugger ended his Giants career with his name splattered across baseball's record book and our memory banks.

The topper was the record-breaking 756th homer on August 7, 2007, as well as six more later to give him 762 overall. And don't forget the record-setting 73 home runs in a blockbuster 2001 season. The four homers, 13 walks, and .471 batting average in the 2002 World Series. The four straight National League MVP awards from 2001–04. The five Gold Gloves to accompany the four from Pittsburgh. The 11th-hour surge to get him into his 14th All-Star Game at the Giants' park his legacy helped build. The rubber chickens fans strung up after his intentional walks. The massive elbow pad. The batter's-box pirouette. The 500–500 club he founded for homers and stolen bases. And, of course, the assorted knee injuries, the arrogant attitude, the clubhouse Barcalounger, the fishy trainers, and the dark, dark cloud of suspicion about his use of performance-enhancing drugs.

ON THE BENCH: Okay, say Bonds has too much baggage for your team, that his legacy is too tainted by possible steroid use and the federal indictment for perjury and obstruction of justice. Then, 1989 National League MVP Kevin Mitchell is a nice alternate, especially if he's willing to make another barehanded catch like the one he did along Busch Stadium's left-field line in '89. Let's also not forget Jeffrey "Hac Man" Leonard, who won MVP honors in the 1987 National League Championship Series loss to St. Louis by belting four homers and introducing America to his one-flap-down home-run trot.

CENTER FIELD: WILLIE MAYS

 If you've got millions of bucks, you can buy the naming rights to a stadium (see: Pac Bell/SBC/AT&T Park). If you've got Willie Mays' credentials, you can have a stadium's address named in your honor. Mays never got to play in the Giants' current home at 24 Willie Mays Plaza (it opened in 2000), but he sure did exceptional work at Candlestick Park, at the Polo Grounds, and everywhere else he put on a Giants uniform.

"The Say Hey Kid" represented the Giants in 22 All-Star Games, and although he won his first MVP award in 1954 when the Giants still played in New York, he won his second in 1965 when he hit a career-best 52 homers for San Francisco's version. Mays was a 12-time Gold Glove centerfielder, a lifetime .302 hitters, and he's the franchise leader in games (2,857), at-bats (10,477), runs (2,011), hits

(3,187), doubles (504), home runs (646), total bases (5,907), and extra-base hits (1,289).

Unlike his godson Barry Bonds, Mays' legacy isn't tainted by any suspicious activity or crass behavior. He's the greatest Giant of them all, and he's the easiest lock when picking a Giants All-Time lineup. He's also one of baseball's most cherished legends, as evident by the reception he received as the guest of honor before the 2007 All-Star Game at AT&T Park.

ON THE BENCH: Picking a bridesmaid to Mays just doesn't seem right. But the top candidates are Billy North (58 steals in 1979), Brett Butler (lots of hustle, lots of hits from 1988–90), Gary Maddux (first three-plus seasons of his 15-year career were in San Francisco), and Darren Lewis (Gold Glove in '94).

RIGHT FIELD: BOBBY BONDS

Of course, without his loins, the Giants' wouldn't have had a second-generation slugger to carry them into this millennium. But before Barry established his record-setting legacy, Bobby had his fine moments, too. Start with his debut on June 25, 1968, when he belted a grand slam to open a 9–0 win over the Dodgers. In the 1973 All-Star Game, he homered, doubled, won MVP honors, and had Sparky Anderson declaring him the best player in America.

Bonds went on in 1973 to almost become baseball's first 40–40 player, stealing 43 bases and hitting 39 home runs. Bonds did follow Willie Mays' lead into the 300–300 club, and he won three Gold Gloves while with the Giants from 1968–74. When Barry joined the Giants in 1993, his father was part of the package, and Bobby served as the most trusted hitting coach (to the game's most feared hitter) before passing away in 2003.

ON THE BENCH: Jack Clark emerged as a mainstay in the heart of the Giants order in 1978, producing 25 home runs, 98 RBIs, a 26-game hit streak, an All-Star berth, and a fifth-place showing in MVP voting. He hit over 20 homers in five seasons, and 20 back then is equivalent to, what, 40 homers now? While he never made it to the postseason in his injury-plagued Giants career, he did reach the playoffs his first year away from them. In the 1985 playoffs with the St. Louis Cardinals, Clark hit a two-out, three-run homer—with first base open—in the top of the ninth for a Game 6 win that clinched the National League Championship Series against the host Dodgers. Anytime anyone with Giants' roots can ruin the Dodgers' day, that's a moment Giants fans will embrace.

PITCHERS: JUAN MARICHAL/ROBB NEN

When it comes to naming a starting pitcher, you've got to start with Marichal, who started off his Hall of Fame career in 1960 by throwing a one-hitter against the Phillies and posting the first of his 52 career shutouts. He went on to win a San Francisco Giants-record 238 games, make nine All-Star teams, and notch 20-win seasons six times from 1960–73. He was on the mound tossing a five-hitter when the Giants won their first National League West title in 1971 with a September 30 win at San Diego.

The right-hander also had among the game's best earned-run averages, as well as a unique, high leg kick in his windup. Unfortunately, video replays of his Giants days (1960–73) usually include one of baseball's darkest moments, when Marichal used his bat to attack Dodgers catcher Johnny Roseboro in 1965. Marichal didn't finish that game, but he did toss 244 complete games, a San Francisco Giants record along with those for innings pitched (3,444), and strikeouts (2,281).

When it comes to closing out a game, call in Nen from the bullpen. Acquiring Nen in 1998 during the Florida Marlins' fire sale was pivotal to the Giants' status as playoff contenders. Nen saved a franchise-high 206 games and virtually gave his right arm for the Giants. The hard-throwing righty, with a devastating slider and mean fast-ball, secretly pitched with pain during the Giants' run to the 2002 World Series. Once there, Nen continued to pitch, even saving Games 1 and 4 before the series-turning loss in Game 6, where he allowed a go-ahead two-run double to Troy Glaus before striking out Adam Kennedy with the last pitch of his career.

That fifth and final season saw Nen tally a career-high 43 saves with a 2.20 ERA in 68 appearances. At age 32, he had become the 16th pitcher to record 300 saves, but he was the youngest to do so. Despite three surgeries on his shredded rotator cuff, Nen couldn't continue and retired in February 2005.

ALSO IN THE ROTATION: Gaylord Perry still wonders what more he could have done for the Giants to prevent them from trading him after the 1971 season. After all, he had posted a 2.96 ERA in his 10 seasons and still ranks second in San Francisco Giants history for wins (134), complete games (125), shutouts (21), innings (2,294.2), and strikeouts (1,606). He won 58 games in his final three Giants campaigns before getting shipped to Cleveland, where he promptly won 24 games in 1972 and captured his first of two Cy Young awards.

ALSO IN THE BULLPEN: Rod Beck, the colorful creature known as "Shooter," was a pretty amazing reliever and terrific guy. That's what made his drug-related death in 2007 so crushing to Giants fans. Beck piled up a then-Giants record 199 saves from 1991–97, with three-time All-Star trips and the 1994 Rolaids Relief Award. His 1997 swan song led to the division championship, as well as a career defining moment on September 18, 1997. That's when he allowed three consecutive singles to load the bases in the top of the 10th against the Dodgers. Beck escaped the jam with a strikeout and a double-play grounder, and Brian Johnson's game-winning homer won it for the Giants in the 12th.

MANAGER: DUSTY BAKER

Yes, Dusty's a former Dodger ("Boo! Boo!"), but, hey, so is Roger Craig. They're also the Giants' top skippers over the past 50 years, and Dusty gets the nod here over Craig. For starters (and a harmless giggle), Dusty won a World Series game, unlike Craig. Actually, Baker's 2002 team won three World Series games before bowing to the Angels. Of course, Dusty also had baseball's biggest bat ever on his side, that of one Barry Lamar Bonds. They both joined the Giants in 1993, missing the postseason that year despite winning a franchise-record 103 games. After back-to-back last place finishes, the Giants rebounded in 1997, winning the West as "The Team of Dustiny." A laid-back dude who'd still flip a switch and stick up for his troops, Dusty guided the Giants to first- or second-place finishes in the NL West in his final six seasons, also winning the division in 2000 and making a wild-card run to the 2002 World Series.

ON THE BENCH: Under Craig's "Humm Baby" regime, the Giants erased their losing mentality and, in 1987, won their first division title since 1971. That initial Craig team also came within a win of the World Series. Craig replaced Jim Davenport toward the end of the 100-loss 1985 season, piloted a group of young prospects into a bona fide pennant

211

contender, and taught his pitchers how devastating a split-finger fastball could be. Craig's 1989 Giants won the National League pennant before getting swept by the A's in the Battle of the Bay. Hey, not even that could crush the "Humm Baby" spirit that encompassed Craig's tenure.

WHICH WERE BONDS' BEST HOME RUNS AS A GIANT?

When Barry Bonds left the Giants after the 2007 season, he stood atop baseball's all-time home-run list with 762 Bondsian blasts. Okay, now let's review each and every one of them. Kidding, kidding. Let's instead replay his 10 best works of art:

10. PASSING RUTH, MAY 28, 2006

This shot, number 715 to pass Babe Ruth, soared to center field, and it was scooped up underneath the bleachers by a fan who was at a concession stand buying beer and pretzels.

9. WALK-OFF WONDERS, AUGUST 2003

His 651st and 652nd home runs were 10th-inning blasts and walk-off winners against the Braves. Those heroic shots came just days before Bobby Bonds died.

8. TYING RUTH, MAY 21, 2006

Bonds pulled even with Ruth by homering across the Bay in Oakland. Well, his homer didn't actually stretch across the water like the Bay Bridge. Rather, it landed about eight rows up from the right-center field wall.

7. GIANT DEBUT, APRIL 12, 1993

In Bonds' first home game with the Giants, he hit a solo home run (number 178 overall in his career) in his first at-bat, giving the Giants a 1–0 lead in an eventual 4–3 win over Florida.

6. THE 700 CLUB, SEPTEMBER 17, 2004

He hit this one off San Diego's Jake Peavy, who also got Bonds to fly out to center in his final at-bat as a Giant on September 26, 2007.

5. THROW 'EM OUT, HIT 'EM OUT, JULY 24, 2003

Bonds preserved a 2–2 tie by throwing out Arizona's Craig Counsell at the plate in the top of the ninth inning. Then, on the first pitch in the bottom of the ninth, Bonds belted his 470th home run in walk-off fashion. Not a bad way to celebrate his 39th birthday. But after the game, he dashed to the hospital to see his ailing father, who died a month later.

4. THE 500 CLUB, APRIL 17, 2001

Bonds entered the exclusive 500-homer club in dramatic fashion, sending Terry Adams's eighth-inning pitch into McCovey Cove and giving the Giants a 3–2 win over the Dodgers. It was the ninth "Splash Hit"—Bonds having hit that waterway first in 2000 against the Mets.

3. (OUT OF THIS) WORLD SERIES, 2002

After homering in his first career World Series at-bat during a Game 1 win, Bonds' second homer showed the world his tape-measure power, a 485-foot shot in the ninth inning of an 11–10 Game 2 loss. A television camera caught an awe-struck Tim Salmon saying in the Angels dugout: "That's the farthest ball I've ever seen hit." Bonds had four home runs and 13 walks in 30 plate appearances in the Series.

2. PASSING MCGWIRE, OCTOBER 5 AND 7, 2001

Yes, home runs numbers 71–73 during the stretch represent more than one homer, but that record-setting trio came in rapid-fire, dramatic succession to cap off the greatest single-season output ever. Bonds broke Mark McGwire's single-season record with his 71st home run off the Dodgers' Chan Ho Park in the bottom of the first inning. Number 72 came two innings later in the eventual 11–10 loss, and number 73 landed on the right-field arcade two days later in the season finale.

1. PASSING HANK, AUGUST, 7, 2007

This was the moment everyone had been waiting for, especially Bonds. He finally passed Hank Aaron atop baseball's home-run list with a majestic, solo shot to right-center field in the fifth inning off Washington Nationals southpaw Mike Bacsik. Bonds, amidst fireworks an unfurling of celebratory banners, then thanked the crowd. But he was upstaged by a surprise video message from Aaron, who offered his prerecorded congratulations on the centerfield screen.

WHICH WERE MAYS' BEST HOME RUNS AS A GIANT?

Willie Mays' most famous moment of his Hall of Fame career is an over-the-shoulder catch in Game 1 of the 1954 World Series, when the Giants still called New York home. Mays was the ultimate five-tool player, though, and of his 660 home runs, here are the top ones from his San Francisco days:

5. 500 CLUB, SEPTEMBER 13, 1965

A solo shot off the Houston Astros' Don Nottebart put Mays in the 500 Home Run Club. It came in the midst of a 14-game win streak, and it was one of a career-high 52 home runs Mays hit en route to his second National League MVP award.

4. FOUR-HOMER GAME, APRIL 30, 1961

Mays went deep in the first, third, sixth and eighth innings, and he very nearly did so in the fifth but had that shot snared at the wall by Hank Aaron, who had two home runs himself that game. Mays nearly had another chance at five homers, but the game ended with him in the on-deck circle.

3. SHUTOUT SNAPPED, JULY 2, 1963

In the bottom of the 16th inning of an epic pitcher's duel at Candlestick, Mays homered off the Milwaukee Braves' Warren Spahn, who pitched a complete game along with the Giants' Juan Marichal. Mays' walk-off shot came with one out, and it went out beyond left field.

2. TOPS IN NL, MAY 4, 1966

Mays eclipsed Mel Ott's National League record for home runs, hitting number 512 in a 6–1 win over the Dodgers before a Candlestick crowd that gave him a rabid ovation. Ott played his entire career for the (New York) Giants and held the National League record for homers since 1937.

1. WORLD SERIES DREAM LIVES; 1962 REGULAR-SEASON FINALE:

Mays' eighth-inning shot off the Houston Colt .45's Turk Farrell gave the Giants a 2–1 win, sending them into a three-game playoff against the Brooklyn Dodgers and eventually the first World Series in San Francisco history.

WHAT WERE THE GIANTS' BEST HOMERS NOT BY BONDS OR MAYS?

The most famous home run in Giants history is undoubtedly Bobby Thompson's "Shot Heard 'Round the World," a three-run homer in the bottom of the ninth that lifted the Giants past the Brooklyn Dodgers in the 1951 regular-season finale. As Russ Hodges called it: "The Giants win the pennant! The Giants win the pennant! The Giants win the pennant!" But those were the New York Giants. Here are the top five homers by San Francisco Giants not named Barry Bonds or Willie Mays:

5. MIKE IVIE, MAY 28, 1978

The first of his two pinch-hit grand slams this season came off Don Sutton, and it sparked a born-again Giants franchise past the Dodgers 6–5. It came on Jacket Day/Italian-American Day in what was then the largest crowd in Giants history. Plus, a listener on the team's then-flagship radio station (KSFO) won a Chevy Chevette thanks to Ivie's slam. Ivie's second pinch-hit granny, by the way, came a month later in the same game in which McCovey hit his 500th home run.

4. WILL CLARK, APRIL 8, 1986

One swing of the bat signified a new era for the Giants. Clark homered in his first-career at-bat, a shot made more legendary by it having come off Nolan Ryan, and it soared to straightaway center field inside the Houston Astrodome. This moment even trumps Clark's grand slam off the Cubs' Greg Maddux in Game 1 of the 1989 NLCS; though his best clutch hit was a two-out, two-run single in Game 5 to clinch the World Series trip.

3. JOE MORGAN, 1982 SEASON FINALE

This two-out, three-run blast over the right-field fence will always serve as a sentimental favorite for Giants fans, and a dagger in the Dodgers' heart. Eliminated from postseason contention two days earlier, the Giants returned the favor by winning this regular-season finale 5–3 and preventing the Dodgers from tying Atlanta for the division title.

2. BRIAN JOHNSON, SEPTEMBER 18, 1997

Locked in a classic pennant race with the Dodgers, Johnson capped the Giants' two-game sweep of their SoCal rivals with a 12th-inning, game-winning home run before a euphoric crowd at Candlestick. It pulled the Giants into a first place tie with the Dodgers, and the Giants never fell from that perch en route to the playoffs.

1. ALL OF WILLIE McCOVEY'S

We simply can't ignore McCovey's 469 home runs with the Giants. What's his best? McCovey laughed and said it's "impossible" to determine because he hit so many. Then he reminisced about career number 500 (in Atlanta, 1978, off Jamie Easterly) and number 512 (passing Mel Ott's 511, at Pittsburgh, 1979, off Grant Jackson). Others might point to one of his 18 grand slams, or perhaps one that cleared Candlestick's fence, and bounced into the parking lot. Now when home runs leave the Giants' ballpark, some fittingly fall into the waterway known as McCovey Cove.

Ted Williams once said the All-Star Game was invented for Willie Mays. Well, then Stu Miller was born to symbolize Candlestick Park's windy reputation. Surely you've heard the tale of Miller getting blown off Candlestick's mound in the 1961 All-Star Game. Well, it's not totally true, but don't let the truth get in the way of a classic Giants' moment.

Candlestick is famous for its swirling winds, and Miller, despite having an incredible change-up, is known more for that wind-aided, All-Star Game balk. With the National League clinging to a 3–2 lead, Miller swayed in the wind and umpires called a ninth-inning balk on him with Rocky Colavito at the plate. Al Kaline went to third, Roger Maris to second, and Kaline later scored the tying run on an error.

No, Miller wasn't blown off the mound. But that's how the myth goes. And it overshadows the facts that, (a) he ended up as the winning pitcher when Willie Mays scored the deciding run in the 10th, and (b) Miller went 14–5 that season.

His memorable All-Star Game moment at least wasn't as nightmarish as Atlee Hammaker's. In 1983 at Comiskey Park, Hammaker allowed the first grand slam in All-Star Game history, a shot to right field by Fred Lynn. That capped a seven-run outburst off Hammaker, whose career would be dogged by shoulder and elbow injuries, not to mention a three-run homer to St. Louis' Jose Oquendo in Game 7 of the 1987 NLCS.

Because of their unique qualities from their lone All-Star appearances, Miller and Hammaker overshadow the Giants' brighter All-Star moments. Specifically, we're talking about the MVP performances of Mays (1963, '68), Juan Marichal (1965), Willie McCovey (1969), and Bobby Bonds (1973).

Barry Bonds played in 11 All-Star Games in his Giants career, going 6–for–31 with two home runs, seven RBIs, four walks, and no MVP accolades. An 11th-hour voting crush got Bonds into the 2007 All-Star Game starting lineup at AT&T Park. After blowing off Giants owner Peter Magowan's request for him to participate in the Home Run Derby, Bonds went a measly 0–for–2 in the All-Star Game and surprisingly exited that grand stage after only three innings. That surely didn't please all those ballot-box stuffers.

Bonds had come and gone in such forgettable fashion. Actually, Bonds' most picturesque moment of that night came when he delicately ushered his godfather, Mays, into a car on the center-field grass during the pregame ceremony.

There wasn't much wind in that 2007 game—officially, 10 miles per hour—so there would be no gusts blowing starters Dan Haren or Jake Peavy off the mound. And that's a good thing. For Miller's moment in 1961 is unique, so much so that it's the top All-Star moment in Giants lore.

GIANTS' BIGGEST WORLD SERIES NEMESIS: RICHARDSON, SPIEZIO, OR THE QUAKE?

In their half century in San Francisco, the Giants don't have a world championship to show for their efforts. Instead, they lug around a 0–for–3 showing in World Series appearances, in 1962, 1989, and 2002. The Giants' first devastating blow was delivered by New York Yankees second baseman Bobby Richardson in Game 7, 1962.

Richardson caught Willie McCovey's line drive to end the 1962 World Series, stranding Matty Alou at third base, and Willie Mays at second. McCovey blistered Yankees pitcher Ralph Terry's 1–1 pitch, but the topspin brought the ball fatally into Richardson's mitt. Great catch by him, bold move by Terry to pitch to McCovey. Not only was first base open, but McCovey already homered off him in Game 2 and tripled earlier in Game 7.

Richardson's name is one Giants fans still hadn't forgotten 45 years later. He drew boos when he was introduced at AT&T Park in 2007 during a reunion of the '62 Yankees and '62 Giants. Richardson took that in stride though, knowing how monumental a play he had made, a moment that Charles Schulz recreated a couple times in his *Peanuts* comic strip.

The next time the Giants made it to the World Series, the A's weren't their only impediment. After losing the first two games in Oakland, the Giants' comeback plans got scuttled. And rattled. And shaken to the earth's core. At 5:04 p.m., a 7.1 magnitude earthquake rocked the Bay Area.

The Series resumed 10 days later, and the A's continued their rout. Could the Giants have contended better if the earthquake didn't interrupt the proceedings? No way. The Giants combined to hit .209 in the Series and couldn't match the A's talent across the board, something quite evident back in the spring training wars Tony La Russa commanded.

As close as the Giants were to winning it all in Game 7 of the '62 World Series, and as great as it would have been to top their Bay Area neighbors in '89, the Giants seemed even closer in 2002, when they were eight outs away from clinching it. But then Dusty Baker pulled starter Russ Ortiz from the mound in favor of Felix Rodriguez. Then Angels second baseman Scott Spiezio suddenly became known in the Bay Area for more than just singing like a rock star when with the A's. Spiezio greeted Rodriguez with a full-count, three-run homer to right field, cutting the Giants lead to 5–3. No, it didn't give the Angels the win, but it was the Series' turning point. The Angels went ahead in the eighth off Darrin Erstad's leadoff homer and Troy Glaus' two-run double, forcing a Game 7 they won 4–1 over the deflated Giants.

If it's any consolation, they have had a World Series hero, in a roundabout way. That would be J.T. Snow, who scooped up manager Dusty Baker's three-year-old son—Darren, a bat boy—near home plate just before David Bell scored in a 16–4, Game 5 rout of the Angels in 2002.

But the wait continues for a World Series title, a wait that really wouldn't seem so long had Richardson missed McCovey's liner in 1962. Yep, that one still stings the most, and that's why Richardson remains the Giants' biggest World Series nemesis.

A'S

WHAT WAS THE BEST HOME RUN IN A'S HISTORY?

Some of baseball's most prolific home-run hitters have called Oakland home. The A's haven't had a "shot heard 'round the world," but they have had more than their share of absurdly long bombs, postseason blasts, and clutch homers. The most famous home run in A's history is, without a doubt, Kirk Gibson's walk-off piece for the Los Angeles Dodgers against Dennis Eckersley in Game 1 of the 1988 World Series. Okay, sorry, A's fans, here are the top five homers from one of your own sluggers:

5. JOSE CANSECO, OCTOBER 7, 1989

This 480-foot blast was the first to reach the Toronto SkyDome's highest (fifth-tier) deck, and that third-inning solo shot gave the A's a 3–0 lead in Game 4 of the 1989 ALCS. A single by Canseco in the seventh brought in the eventual winning run.

4. MARK MCGWIRE, OCTOBER 18, 1988

Beware, this isn't the one that soared 537 feet into the Seattle Kingdome's upper deck off Randy Johnson in

1997. Nor is it one of his two 16th inning blasts in back-to-back games that lifted the A's on July 3 and 4, 1988. Nor is it a walk-off grand slam against Boston in 1990. But this one, off the Dodgers' Jay Howell, did end Game 3 of the 1988 World Series.

3. GENE TENACE, OCTOBER 4, 1972

The A's 1970s dynasty got off to an improbable start when, in Game 1 of the 1972 World Series, Tenace hit a two-out homer to left in the second inning for a 1–0 lead. He wasn't done, though. He also homered in his next at-bat, a fifth-inning shot that gave the A's a 3–2 lead they kept to stun the Big Red Machine. Tenace had only one hit in 17 at-bats in the ALCS vs. Detroit. He also had only five home runs in the regular season, but he delivered four in that '72 World Series.

2. SCOTT HATTEBERG, SEPTEMBER 4, 2002

The A's set an American League record with 20 straight victories when Hatteberg hit a pinch-hit home run in the bottom of the ninth for a 12–11 win over the Kansas City Royals. What made his shot to right field more incredible is that the A's led 11–0 through three innings before the Royals tied it at 11 in the top of the ninth.

1. REGGIE JACKSON, JULY 13, 1971

Dock Ellis delivered the pitch in the All-Star Game, and Jackson slammed it on to Tiger Stadium's roof, where the titanic blast was stopped by an electrical transformer at the base of a light tower. It came on a 0–2 pitch, and it prompted Wayne State researchers to study its flight path to determine just how far it could have gone. Some say over 500 feet. Some even say 650. Just say it put the baseball world on notice that the A's would be packing a punch in the 1970s.

IN BILLY BEANE WE TRUST, STILL?

A's fans have long conditioned themselves to this scenario: A budding prospect emerges into a superstar, then disappears from the low-budget A's clubhouse, and cashes in elsewhere. Many players have gone via free agency, and many, many, many have received a cell phone call from General Manager Billy Beane, informing them they've been traded.

This should tell you a lot about Beane's tenure since becoming the A's GM in October 1997: His bio takes up one page in the A's 2007 media guide, and then the next two pages list the trades he's made. After shipping away the A's best pitcher (Dan Haren, 2007 All-Star Game starter) and one of their best hitters (Nick Swisher) prior to the 2008 season, Beane received more criticism than usual from A's fans, who wondered if this cycle of player departures will ever end or if the A's are indeed a major league farm system. The A's responded, at least initially, with one of their best Aprils in several years and talk of "rebuilding" was replaced by thoughts of "contending."

Sure, Beane still has A's fans' trust. Five playoff runs in 10 seasons gives a man plenty of credibility. So does his history of making beneficial trades. He's willing to part with a red-hot player a year too early rather than a year too late, which is the same strategy Bill Walsh employed during the 49ers' 1980 dynasty.

Even when Swisher, the face of the franchise, got dealt to the Chicago White Sox after the 2007 season, he called Beane "a genius" based on that history of suave personnel moves. A few years earlier, Michael Lewis' best-selling book *Moneyball* shed amazing light on how Beane conducted business, and it further gained fans' trust in the methods to Beane's madness.

He insists it's no fun to cut ties with players like Swisher and Haren, and he hopes an improved revenue situation will sink that ferry. That said, it's in his restless personality to constantly try improving the franchise, and that's what every fan should want out of their general manager.

And, yes, it still stings A's fans to see so many stars shoot elsewhere under Beane's watch, including pitchers Tim Hudson and Mark Mulder, both traded away in a three-day span in December 2004. Haren came to the A's as part of the Mulder deal, however, and so did Daric Barton, the 2008 A's Opening Day first baseman.

The hope, among Beane and A's fans, is that the team's payroll will increase substantially when, or if, the team opens its new ballpark village just south of Oakland in Fremont. The 32,000-seat Cisco Field is slated to open in 2012, though environmental impact reports and public transit questions could seriously hinder plans.

The proposed ballpark at least adds a new twist to the A's constant rebuilding efforts. Few seem sure it will get built. But few also are willing to doubt Beane's methods to constantly rework the roster and farm system, so, until further notice (or further trades), in Beane we trust.

WHAT WAS CHARLIE FINLEY'S BEST GIMMICK WITH THE A'S?

76 Once upon a time, baseball didn't use steroid-enhanced sluggers to attract fans. Instead, former A's owner Charles O. Finley came up with other methods to stir up interest. Sure, he could spot on-field talent. But he also created sideshows, the kind you'd never expect from today's stodgy baseball owners (but perhaps current Dallas Mavericks owner Mark Cuban).

Finley bought the Kansas City A's in 1960, moved them to Oakland in 1968, and sold them to the Haas family in 1980. Those 20 years saw a parade of outlandish innovation, not to mention his squabbles over salary with star players and his benching of second baseman Mike Andrews in the 1973 World Series.

Bring up Finley's gimmicks and people will smile as they recall the mechanical rabbit that popped up with baseballs for the plate umpire. More smiles will come at the mention of "Hot Pants Day," when women in hot pants got in free. Of course there's also "Charlie O," Finley's mule that he often paraded before crowds (although he was barred from bringing out the mule before a Raiders game when coach John Madden was informed of that distracting plot.)

Some of Finley's ideas worked: Green-and-gold uniforms, white cleats, the designated hitter, and nighttime World Series games.

Some didn't work: Orange baseballs, the three-ball walk, and the designated runner, a role given in 1974 to sprinter Herb Washington, who never batted or played in the field.

Finley also made his coaches (including Joe DiMaggio) wear white hats, while players wore green ones. He gave players nicknames, including Jim "Catfish" Hunter and John "Blue Moon" Odom.

But the best gimmick or promotional tool from Finley's funhouse was...The Mustache. Reggie Jackson showed up with one for the 1972 season, a few other players got into the act, and then Finley offered each player $300 if they donned mustaches for "Mustache Day." The unconventional look stuck, and it was a symbol of unity in a clubhouse known for brawling teammates and their disgust for Finley. The Mustache Gang was born, as was a dynasty that won three straight World Series titles, from 1972–74.

WHO ARE THE ALL-TIME BEST A'S?

CATCHER: TERRY STEINBACH

From homering in his first major league at-bat as a September 1986 callup, to homering in his final at-bat with the A's 10 years later, Steinbach delivered plenty of special moments. He was the A's backstop in three World Series, and he made three All-Star Games, most notably a 1988 appearance that critics thought was undeserving, at least until he won MVP honors by homering off Dwight Gooden with a bat that misspelled his name as "Steinbeck."

Steinbach didn't just hit well: He rarely made an error, he could throw out baserunners and—better him than us—he served as a player rep during the 1994 strike. Steinbach not only caught the A's three straight American League-pennant teams from 1988–90, he was also behind the plate on Dave Stewart's no-hitter in 1990. In the 1989 World Series, he hit a three-run homer to seal the A's Game 2 win, but the real lasting image came before Game 3 when cameras focused in on him consoling his wife after the massive earthquake. His most productive offensive season was his 1996 swan song with 100 RBIs and 35 home runs (34 as a catcher, setting an American League record).

ON THE BENCH: Ray Fosse may have had his shoulder wrecked by Pete Rose in a famous 1970 All-Star Game collision, but he still had plenty left to offer the A's in three seasons, including their World Series campaigns of 1973 and '74. Fosse appeared in 141 games in 1973, and he also went yard in the 1974 World Series, hitting a solo homer in the Game 5 finale against the Dodgers. Although Gene Tenace split time at first base and catcher, we'll give him a tip o' the cap in this category, for he was the A's catcher when he hit four home runs and .348 to key the 1972 World Series upset over Cincinnati's Big Red Machine.

FIRST BASE: MARK MCGWIRE

Sorry, but we're here to talk about the past, specifically McGwire's tenure with the A's from 1986–97. He stopped the A's revolving door at first base and became a power-hitting sensation. How he obtained that power is now highly suspect, especially after his Bash Brother, Jose Canseco, claimed to have injected McGwire with steroids in a bathroom stall in the A's clubhouse. Mac went mum on Capitol Hill in 2005 during hearings about steroid use, and his legacy may forever be tainted.

Launching that legacy was his 1987 Rookie of the Year campaign. He hit a single-season rookie record 49 homers and drew the first of his nine All-Star selections as an Athletic. His home-run totals for the following seasons: 32 in 1988, then 33, 39, 22, 42—pause here, for the nine homers in each of his injury-plagued seasons in 1993 and '94—then 52 in '95, his final full season with the A's. Mac had 34 homers in 105 games before being traded during the 1997 season to St. Louis, where he belted a then-record 70 homers in 1998 to eclipse Roger Maris's mark of 61 in '61.

Of McGwire's 583 career homers, 363 were from his A's days, and that doesn't include postseason home runs, the best of which was a Game 3 walk-off clout against the Dodgers' Jay Howell for the A's only win in the 1988 World Series. Did you know: McGwire had six errors in 16 games as a third baseman in his 1996 callup? He then developed into a Gold Glove-winning first baseman. Hall of Fame voters, however, have frowned upon his .263 lifetime batting average, his ability to collect only 1,626 hits (36 percent were homers) and, of course, his alleged use of steroids.

ON THE BENCH: With McGwire mentoring him in his first few seasons, Jason Giambi accomplished something that eluded McGwire—winning MVP honors. The personable Giambi earned the 2000 American League MVP award with a career-high 43 home runs (including four grand slams), and 137 RBIs. He developed into a much better hitter than McGwire, raising his average from .256 as a rookie to .342 by his sixth and final year with the A's, in 2001. Unfortunately, steroids also cast a dark shadow over Giambi's accolades, as he reportedly admitted his steroid use to a federal grand jury during the BALCO scandal. He's not as scorned as McGwire, though, and maybe that's because, (1) he's apologized to America, and, (2), his A's memories are still fresh in our minds, such as his walk-off home run that capped a three-game sweep of the Yankees in 2001.

SECOND BASE: MARK ELLIS

By the end of only his fourth full season with the A's, Ellis established himself as Oakland's premier second baseman. He hits, he fields, and he's been vastly underrated as an all-around gem on the diamond. In Ellis' 2007 season, he set franchise records for a second baseman with 19 home runs as well as a 102-game error-less streak. He also picked a nice way to surpass Dick Green's Oakland record for home runs by a second baseman, doing so with a grand slam against the Giants.

Ellis' .997 field percentage in 2006 set a major league record among second basemen, but he got snubbed out of a Gold Glove, which went to the Royals' Mark Grudzielanek (.994). Of the 632 chances that came Ellis' way in 2006, only two resulted in an error. And he bounces back: two years earlier, Ellis missed the entire season with a shoulder injury he sustained in spring training. It almost ended his career. It didn't, though, and he's responded with the best production ever by an Oakland A's second baseman.

ON THE BENCH: It's been said that if Dick Green hadn't gone 0–for–13 in the 1974 World Series, he would have won MVP honors instead of Rollie Fingers. That's how spectacular Green played second base, not only in that series, but in his career, which ended after that '74 series full of acrobatic dives and double-play turns. He had a .983 career fielding percentage as a second baseman, which is a tad lower than Ellis' .989 mark through 2007. Green's fielding helped compensate for what could be a cool bat (see: .190 batting average in 1970).

80 SHORTSTOP: BERT CAMPANERIS

You could say the A's 1970s dynasty started with Campy Campaneris, for he led off their batting order and provided sparks, speed, versatility, and occasional power. In his nine years in Oakland, he was a five-time All-Star and averaged 44 stolen bases a season. He never stole a base that didn't need to be stolen, and he could have had much bigger stats. Campy actually broke in with the Kansas City A's in 1965, during which he became the first player to play every position in one game. When the A's came west, he came through with a sensational 1968 season featuring a league-leading 177 hits and 62 steals.

During the Oakland A's run to their first World Series, Campy had a notorious moment: He threw his bat at Tigers pitcher Lerrin LaGrow, whose pitch hit Campy in the ankle during Game 2 of the ALCS. Campy had three hits, two steals, and two runs before getting ejected for the incident and suspended for the rest of the ALCS. Campy did use his bat for other postseason memories: Homering to lead off Game 2 of the 1973 ALCS against the Orioles, winning Game 3 of that series with an 11th inning homer, and homering in Game 7 of the 1973 World Series.

OFF THE BENCH: Miguel Tejada makes for an exceptionally strong challenger to Campy, and he even has a 2002 American League MVP award in his corner. That honor came after he hit .308, belted 34 homers, and led the A's to their second division title in three years. So what happened next? Good question. The Mitchell Report, regarding baseball's performance-enhancing drug era, named Tejada as a steroid recipient in 2003, his final season with the A's before leaving for the Orioles' riches. Tejada did hit over 30 homers three straight seasons between 2000–02, the highlight being a three-run shot vs. Minnesota in 2002 that pushed an A's win streak to 18. And he eclipsed the 100-RBI mark in each of his final four A's seasons. But "Miggy" still can't trump "Campy" when it comes to ranking A's shortstops.

THIRD BASE: SAL BANDO

Captain Sal never hit .300 in his prolonged A's career, but he came through in clutch situations so many times. Take Game 2 of the 1983 ALCS, when his second home run of the game was a two-run shot to break open a 3–2 game in the eighth inning. Aside from his swift ability to drive in runs (his 796 RBIs are more than Jose Canseco's or Reggie Jackson's A's totals), Bando kept those wild 1970s teams together. He ran the clubhouse, teased Jackson when needed, and banded his teammates together when A's owner Charlie Finley hated on second baseman Mike Andrews in the 1973 World Series. Runner-up for league MVP in 1971 behind teammate Vida Blue, Bando also finished third in MVP voting in 1974, and fourth in '73.

OFF THE BENCH: Remember back in that 1988 run when Carney Lansford was hitting .400 into July? Or when he would make absurd catches in the Coliseum's vast foul territory? Or when he simply flexed his leadership? Lansford, a South Bay native, was a lifetime .290 hitter and had a strong 10-year run with the A's from 1983–92. A thumb injury derailed his .400 bid in 1988, but he did make the All-Star team before finishing with a .279 clip. He hit .336 in 1989, which was second best in the American League, and then he hit .444 in the postseason run to the world championship. Another A's stud has been Eric Chavez, who reeled off six straight Gold Glove seasons between 2001–06. Chavez's typical annual production has been 30 homers and 100 RBIs, but those numbers have tailed off in recent seasons, and he hit just .222 in his first five postseasons. Did you know: Chavez is the first player to hit for the cycle at the Coliseum, doing so in a 10–3 win over Baltimore on June 21, 2000?

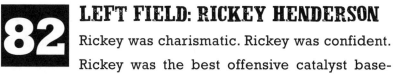

82 LEFT FIELD: RICKEY HENDERSON

Rickey was charismatic. Rickey was confident. Rickey was the best offensive catalyst baseball's ever seen. He was one-of-a-kind, and he had four tours of duty with the A's during his 25-year career. The Oakland Tech High School product began wowing A's fans with his leadoff-hitting, base-stealing exploits during his initial stint from 1979–84. He swiped over 100 bags in three of his first five seasons, including 130 in 1982 as "BillyBall" drew to a close.

He also hit like no other leadoff man. His slew of game-opening homers included one to start a Game 4 victory that clinched the 1989 World Series. Rickey left baseball with more stolen bases (1,406) and runs (2,295) than anyone, as well as the record for walks, which Barry Bonds eventually eclipsed. But before Rickey was done, he won the 1990 American League MVP award, he passed Lou Brock atop the all-time stolen base list in 1991 ("Today I am the greatest of all time!"), and he stole 66 bases at age 39 in 1998, his final A's season.

ON THE BENCH: Joe Rudi's leaping catch at the Riverfront Stadium wall in Game 2 of the 1972 World Series is one of the greatest in A's history. But Rudi was more than that. A three-time All-Star and three-time Gold Glover, he was also an MVP candidate during the A's 1970s dynasty, finishing runner-up in the voting in '72 and '74. In Game 5 of the A's World Series-clinching win over the Dodgers, it

243

was Rudi who put the A's ahead. He homered into the left-field seats to lead off the bottom of the seventh inning, and the Coliseum fans responded by feverishly waving their white pennants.

83 CENTER FIELD: DAVE HENDERSON

"Hendu" arrived in Oakland in 1988 and reenergized his career two years after hitting a game-winning home run off the Angels' Donnie Moore in the 1986 ALCS for the Red Sox. Hendu hit a career-high .304 with 24 homers and 94 RBIs in his inaugural Athletics season, and he actually hit over 20 homers in four of his five full seasons with the A's. A brief member of the Giants during their 1987 season pennant chase, Hendu helped crush the 1989 Giants' World Series dreams by hitting .308 for the A's. He had a monster Game 3 in that World Series, going 3–for–4 with two home runs and four RBIs in a 13–7 win.

Fourteen years after the Seattle Mariners made him a first-round draft pick, Hendu made his first and only All-Star Game, the 1991 Midsummer Classic, which he started alongside Rickey Henderson and Ken Griffey Jr. He hit a career-best 25 home runs that season, and he had well entrenched himself as a fan favorite, especially with the center-field bleacher bums in "Henduland."

ON THE BENCH: Dwayne Murphy provided Gold Glove-winning defense for the A's from 1980–85, and while he wasn't the best hitter (.246 lifetime), he did knock 33

244

homers in 1984 to finish third in the American League. He'd line up in shallow center before using his great reaction skills and instincts to shag flies with the best of them. Murphy was the catalyst in one of baseball's best outfields, as he was flanked in 1979–82 by Rickey Henderson and Tony Armas. Another quality center fielder in A's lore is Billy North, whose speed and stolen-base ability helped the A's get to the 1973 and '74 World Series. An ankle injury sidelined North in the '73 postseason, and he went just 2–for–43 in the '74 and '75 playoffs.

RIGHT FIELD: REGGIE JACKSON

Before he was anointed "Mr. October," before he had a candy bar named after him, before he took New York like Godzilla, Reggie owned Oakland's spotlight. In 1969—the A's second season in Oakland—he swatted a career-high 47 home runs, touted a .608 slugging percentage, drove in 10 runs in one game at Fenway, and made a *Sports Illustrated* cover beneath the headline "Power and Poverty in Oakland." Jackson sure did pack a wallop in what became a priceless Hall of Fame career.

He sat out the A's 1972 World Series trip, but for good reason. He injured his hamstring stealing home for the tying run in an eventual Game 5 win at Detroit, sending the A's into the World Series against Cincinnati. Jackson's 1973 season resulted in American League and World Series MVP honors. He hit .310 in that World Series against the

245

Mets, capped by a two-run homer in the A's Game 7 victory. He homered, too, in the A's next World Series game, a Game 1 win over the Dodgers in 1974.

While his speed and power thrilled fans, don't forget about his outfield presence. Specifically, he started an all-time classic relay that clinched the 1974 World Series: Jackson to second baseman Dick Green to third baseman Sal Bando, to nail a head-first diving Bill Buckner, the potential tying run in Game 5.

ON THE BENCH: We've already penciled in Jose Canseco as the A's top designated hitter, so when it comes to naming a backup to Jackson in right field, how about Tony Armas? He hit 35 homers in 1980, made the 1981 All-Star team and hit .545 in the 1981 playoff-opening series against Kansas City. What about Mike Davis? Yes, another reliable right fielder, but, hey, he homered as a Dodger against the A's in the 1988 World Series finale. Even worse, Davis walked (and stole second) just before Kirk Gibson won Game 1 by going deep off Dennis Eckersley.

 DESIGNATED HITTER: JOSE CANSECO

Okay, so it turns out he was juiced. But baseball's self-proclaimed steroid godfather sure provided some thrills in his playing days, which seemed so innocent and drug free back in the late 1980s and early 1990s. He was the American League MVP in 1988, the first of three straight seasons in which the A's reached the

World Series. More famous than his MVP award in that '88 campaign was his 40/40 feat, as he became the first ballplayer to total 40 home runs (actually 42) and 40 stolen bases in a season. He followed that up by belting three home runs in the A's ALCS sweep of the Red Sox, after which Mark McGwire proclaimed: "Jose Canseco is God." Well, he was a baseball freak who hit tape-measure homers, ran like the wind in that ever-bulking body and knew how to attract attention, such as his fling with Madonna or his ramming of a Porsche into his then-wife Esther's BMW. In his last World Series with the A's, Canseco hit only .083 and got benched in Game 4, leading to Esther calling A's manager Tony La Russa a "punk." Canseco also made an infamous exit from the A's, getting called back from the on-deck circle when he got traded to the Texas Rangers in 1992.

ON THE BENCH: No one's served as the A's designated hitter for more games than Dave Kingman, who finished his 16-year career with three seasons on the A's. He averaged 33 home runs and 101 RBIs from 1984–86. He also had a couple long balls lodge into the rafters in Minnesota and Seattle, and, as sportswriters haven't forgotten, he once sent a dead rat in a box to a press box. A more recent DH candidate is Frank Thomas, who delivered a team-high 39 home runs and 114 RBIs in 2006. Thomas helped spark their American League Division Series sweep of Minnesota, but then went 0–for–13 against the Detroit Tigers in the ALCS.

86 PITCHERS: JIM "CATFISH" HUNTER/DENNIS ECKERSLEY

Catfish Hunter anchored the A's pitching staffs on their World Series teams from 1972–74, going 4–0 in World Series starts and even notching a save in Game 1 of the '74 series against the Dodgers. He parlayed his exceptional control into 20-win seasons each of his final four years with the A's, capped off with a 25–12 campaign and a 2.49 ERA during his run to the 1974 Cy Young Award.

Catfish was exceptionally flawless in 1968, when he pitched the only perfect game in A's history, on May 8 against the Minnesota Twins. Once he gained his freedom from Charlie Finley, he fled in 1975 for the Yankees, with whom he spent the final five seasons of his career. Inducted into the Hall of Fame in 1987, Hunter died in 1999 at the age of 53. While Hunter is our choice for the A's top starter, another Hall of Famer, Eckersley, gets our call out of the bullpen for top closer.

It seems like only yesterday Eckersley was raising his right arm in celebration as the A's completed a four-game sweep of the Boston Red Sox and headed for the 1988 World Series. Eck won MVP honors in that ALCS, saving each of the A's four games. Even after his most famous pitch resulted in Kirk Gibson's walk-off home run in Game 1 of the 1988 World Series, Eck continued down a path that led him to the Hall of Fame.

He averaged an incredible 44 saves per season from 1988–92, including 51 saves and a 1.91 earned-run average in '92 en route to the American League's Cy Young and MVP awards. Not bad for a 41-year-old. Eckersley arrived in Oakland in 1987, freshly sober and intensely determined to reverse a sinking career (6–11, 4.57 ERA in 1986 with the Cubs). Eckersley eventually accepted manager Tony La Russa's use of him as a sidearm-slinging closer and went on to own the ninth inning. When George Thorogood's Bad to the Bone hit the stadium speakers, out came Eck, with the hair, the fist pump, and the nasty control. His crowning moment as a reliever came at the end of the 1989 World Series, when he saved Game 4 in 1–2–3 fashion to complete the sweep of the cross-bay Giants. Actually, the true crowning came in 2004 when he was inducted into the Hall of Fame.

ALSO IN THE ROTATION: Homegrown star Dave Stewart keyed the A's World Series runs from 1988–90, earning MVP honors in the 1989 World Series by winning Games 1 and 3. The following year, Stew no-hit the Toronto Blue Jays on June 29, 1990, the same day Dodger icon Fernando Valenzuela no-hit St. Louis. Stewart's stare is legendary, as is his Game 4 effort (four hits, seven innings) against the Red Sox that vaulted the A's to their first World Series.

Others in the A's dream rotation: Vida Blue, Ken Holtzman, and any one of the A's "Three Aces"—Tim Hudson, Mark Mulder, or 2002 Cy Young winner Barry Zito.

Bob Welch, the 1990 American League Cy Young winner with a 27–6 record, also could enter that debate.

ALSO IN THE BULLPEN: As it says on Rollie Fingers' Hall of Fame plaque, he epitomized the emergence of the modern day relief ace. He and his handlebar mustache were unmistakable trademarks to the A's 1970s dynasty. Fingers saved two games in each of the A's three straight World Series appearances, finishing with MVP honors in the 1974 World Series. The following year, Fingers, Vida Blue, Glenn Abbott, and Paul Lindblad no-hit the Angels, marking the first time four pitchers combined on a major league no-hitter. Fingers and Blue had another memorable outing against the Angels back in 1971, when Blue struck out 17 in the first 11 innings and Fingers struck out seven in the next seven innings of an eventual 1–0, 20-inning win.

MANAGER: TONY LA RUSSA

Dick Williams led the Oakland A's to their first two World Series titles in 1972 and '73, and 35 years later landed in the Hall of Fame. But the nod for the A's top manager goes to one of his former bit players and utility infielders, La Russa.

La Russa has evolved into the third-winningest manager ever, and A's fans won't forget the success their feisty skipper brought the blossoming franchise from 1986–95. An intense strategist, La Russa led the A's to three straight

American League titles from 1988–90, posting the majors' best record each season.

While his 1988 and 1990 teams got humbled in the World Series, he did do a stellar job of keeping an injury plagued 1989 team on track, and that club delivered a World Series sweep of the cross-bay Giants. Anchoring that era weren't just the "Bash Brothers" of Mark McGwire and Jose Canseco, but also Dennis Eckersley, whom La Russa converted into a ninth-inning, Cooperstown-bound closer.

La Russa has been a pillar in the community, and he's remained so during his tenure with the St. Louis Cardinals. He and his family have kept a home in the East Bay town of Alamo, and his Animal Rescue Foundation is very well respected. His longevity with the A's, not to mention his obvious success, has La Russa atop Oakland's all-time list for games managed (1,471) and victories (798).

ON THE BENCH: Williams' stay may have been only three years, but he delivered first-place efforts each season and, of course, won Oakland's first two World Series titles in 1972 and '73.

When Williams came aboard in 1971, he was Finley's 11th manager in 11 years, and he overcame Finley's meddlesome ways and somehow kept his brawling teams focused on the world championship. Managing under Charlie Finley's ownership was a heck of a lot harder than La Russa had it under the Haas family, and Williams had enough by the end of 1973. Williams' .603 winning percentage remains the best of any A's manager, including the franchise's first, legendary Connie Mack (.482). When Williams gained entry into the Hall of Fame in December 2007, he described his managerial style as being firm, tough, and demanding perfection. Yes, he only coached the A's for three seasons, "but three years with Charlie set a record," Williams said in that Hall of Fame press conference.

COLLEGES

WERE CAL'S FIVE LATERALS LEGAL IN THE PLAY?

 If you're a Cal fan, The Play absolutely was legit, and thus the Bears rightly won the 1982 Big Game against Stanford on a five-lateral, band-smashing kickoff return for a touchdown. If you're a Stanford fan, you disagree so vehemently that you're glad to see the 1982 result changed out on The Axe's plaque whenever Stanford wins the Big Game.

The most common debate about The Play is whether Dwight Garner's right knee hit the turf before lateral number three went airborne. If so, The Play should have been whistled dead as Stanford defenders stopped Garner at the Bears' 49-yard line. But because the official's view was blocked, The Play continued. And continued.

Before The Play began, Stanford thought it had the victory in hand, courtesy of a field goal that put the Cardinal ahead 20–19 with four seconds remaining. On the ensuing kickoff, Mark Harmon squib kicked the ball and Kevin Moen retrieved it for Cal near the Bears' 45-yard line. Moen started right, shifted left, and then tossed the ball to Richard Rodgers.

Rodgers took a couple steps before flipping the ball back to Dwight Garner at the Cal 45. The Bears were treading water, but they were still afloat.

Garner churned straight ahead into that pack of white jerseys, and soon Stanford's band spilled on to the field, figuring Garner had been tackled. But then came the third lateral, a toss to Rodgers, who advanced the ball into Stanford territory before dishing it to Mariet Ford.

On the final lateral , Ford was at the Stanford 27 when he tossed the ball FORWARD to Kevin Moen, who caught it at the Stanford 25. A forward lateral is illegal. Right? If so, then Moen's run to the end zone—and into trombonist Gary Tyrrell—should be stricken from the record. On the 25th anniversary of The Play, a video replay was shown to the Pac-10 Conference's supervisor of instant replay, and Verle Sorgen's informal review for the Bay Area News Group concluded that The Play should have been illegal. While Sorgen said he wasn't sure if Gordon's knee was down, he said Ford's lateral "clearly appears forward" and that could be the case for reversing The Play.

But 25 years earlier, all officials could do was confer with each other, and then they ruled that The Play was legal and so was the result: Cal 25, Stanford 20. That score changes to "Stanford 20, Cal 19" whenever Stanford owns The Axe and the accompanying plaque, on which the score is scratched out and altered. It's a ritual that started after Stanford's 1984 victory.

The Play ended John Elway's Stanford career, and, at the time, he called The Play "a farce" and "an insult to college football." Upon The Play's 25th anniversary, Elway broke a long silence about it and said people "can sit there and argue if (Garner's) knee was down until you're blue in the face."

Of course, if you're wearing blue, you're a Cal fan, and you're still celebrating the greatest play in sports history.

WHAT WAS THE BAY AREA'S BEST "MARCH MADNESS" MOMENT?

 We pick this debate up from 1985 on, when the NCAA men's basketball tournament expanded to 64 teams, though we should note the field bumped up to 65 in 2001 with a play-in game.

Stanford's men's program has enjoyed several tournament trips in the past 15 years, and its most exciting moment came in the 1998 Elite Eight. A frantic, last-minute rally by the Cardinal (and a dunking Mark Madsen) resulted in a 79–77 win over Rhode Island and a trip to the Final Four, where third-seeded Stanford lost to Kentucky 86–85 in overtime.

But Stanford's high seed disqualifies it from winning our argument. Cinderella upsets define "March Madness," so let's look at those. Two Bay Area programs nearly provided epic "Madness" upsets. There was the 1997 St. Mary's team that hung tight with Tim Duncan's Wake Forest squad before falling 68–46. In 1996, San Jose State made a run at becoming the first 16th seed to knock off a top seed. The Spartans trailed by only six at halftime of an eventual 110–72 blowout loss to ultimate champion Kentucky.

But these efforts can't hold a candle to the 1993 Tournament. So who pulled off the bigger upset, 15th-seeded Santa Clara over second-seeded Arizona in the first round, or sixth-seeded Cal over two-time defending champion Duke (the third seed) in the second round?

The Santa Clara Broncos were 20-point underdogs when they stunned Lute Olson's Arizona Wildcats 64–61, only the second time ever a 15th seed had knocked off a second seed. Helping clinch that upset was a freshman guard from Canada (a future two-time NBA MVP) named Steve Nash, who hit six straight clutch free throws in the final minute. Pete Eisenrich scored 19 points for the Broncos under Coach Dick Davey, the first of his 15 seasons at Santa Clara.

Arizona went on a 25–0 run at one point but, in the end, after Damon Stoudamire missed at the buzzer, the Wildcats endured a first-round exit for the second straight year. They also bowed out quickly in 1992 to 14th-seeded East Tennessee State.

Because of that repeated failure by Arizona, it could bolster the argument that Cal's 82–73 upset over Duke was bigger. In it, Cal freshman Jason Kidd won a duel with Duke senior point guard Bobby Hurley, as Kidd tallied a school record 14 assists and landed on the Sports Illustrated cover. Lamond Murray put up a double-double for Cal with a team-high 28 points and 10 assists.

Helping motivate Cal were critical words from LSU coach Dale Brown. After Cal beat 11th-seeeded LSU 66–64 in the first round on an acrobatic shot by Kidd in the final seconds, Brown said in the postgame press conference that Cal didn't have "a prayer" against Duke. They not only had a prayer, they had themselves the second-best March Madness upset in Bay Area history. Although Santa Clara, like Duke, also bowed out in the second round of that 1993 tournament (losing to Temple), the Broncos had already shocked the world and broken more brackets by virtue of their first-round upset of Arizona, the Bay Area's best March Madness moment.

Bonus: What's the Bay Area's worst "March Madness" moment?

We give the nod here to the Cardinal. Aside from a 2001 trip to the Elite Eight as a number-one seed, Stanford failed to get past the second round in 11 of 14 tourney trips between 1989–2007, including second-round defeats as a top seed in 2000 (to Final Four-bound North Carolina), and in 2004 (to Alabama). The Cardinal was a third seed in 2008 when it did get past the second round, only to fall 82–62 to second-seeded Texas in the Round of 16. Stanford's string of disappointment started off in 1989, when the Cardinal bowed out as a three seed in the first round to Sienna, abruptly ending Stanford's first NCAA Tournament appearance in 47 years. After another first-round loss in 1992, Coach Mike Montgomery's program rebounded to make 10 straight NCAA tourneys from 1995–2004.

But Monty's last team went out with a huge thud, falling as a top seed to Alabama 70–67 in the second round in Seattle. That, folks, takes the cake here. It not only marked Monty's final game before his failed jump to the NBA (and 2008 surprising hop to rival Cal), it also concluded a 30–2 season that had only one other loss (at nearby Washington two weeks earlier), and one terrific buzzer-beating win over Arizona, a victory Tiger Woods celebrated courtside at Maples Pavilion instead of playing at the AT&T Pebble Beach National Pro-Am.

WAS CAL'S 2007 COLLAPSE THE BIGGEST EVER IN COLLEGE FOOTBALL?

In a season filled with college football upsets, none would have been bigger in 2007 than had Cal actually finished atop a national poll for the first time since 1937. Cal was in the midst of national-title contention when, wham-o, it lost six of its last seven regular-season games.

It definitely will go down as one of the all-time busts in Cal's storied history. But, thanks to a comeback win in what normally should be considered a meaningless bowl game, the Bears saved some face, unbelievably, with a 42–36 Armed Forces Bowl triumph over Air Force. But the Bears' freefall was fast and furious before that finale.

The Bears' 2007 fortunes flipped just as dusk settled in at Memorial Stadium on October 13. That's when the second-ranked Bears were on the cusp of moving up in the polls, having heard by halftime that top-ranked LSU just lost in overtime to Kentucky. Cal was less than 15 minutes away from a probable top ranking as it took a 21–20 lead at the start of the fourth quarter against Oregon State. But the Beavers rallied, and they prevailed when time ran out on a last-ditch drive by the Bears, the final play coming on a boneheaded scramble by Cal quarterback Kevin Riley to the Beavers' 10-yard line.

Cal fell to 5–1, then kept falling. They lost at UCLA and Arizona State, won 20–17 over a hapless Washington State team, then finished the regular season with losses at home to USC and on the road at Washington and rival Stanford.

That horrendous finish wiped away the good vibes that came with a season-opening win over Tennessee and a rare win at Oregon.

But the Bears were still able to embellish their 7–6 record, noting how it was their sixth straight winning season in as many years under Coach Jeff Tedford. Old Blues, however, believe the second-half collapse could have been avoided if Tedford had benched starting quarterback Nate Longshore in favor of Riley. Yes, the same Riley who faltered on the final play of the Oregon State loss. But also the same Riley who rallied them against Air Force, replacing Longshore in the second quarter and completing 16 of 19 passes for 269 yards and three touchdowns, plus a rushing touchdown.

Considering how long those Old Blues have waited for Cal to return to the top of a poll, forgive them if they think 2007 was the biggest collapse ever.

But it really wasn't, when you look at the grand scheme of NCAA football. In the final nine weeks of the 2007 season, second-ranked teams went 2–7, including losses by USC, South Florida, Boston College, Oregon, Kansas, West Virginia, and, of course, Cal. In a cruel twist of fate, it was second-ranked LSU that ended up winning the BCS Championship Game over top-ranked Ohio State.

WAS STANFORD'S WIN OVER USC COLLEGE FOOTBALL'S GREATEST UPSET EVER?

91 As a 41-point underdog, Stanford pulled off clearly the largest upset in terms of a point spread on October 6, 2007. At the Los Angeles Coliseum, the Cardinal rallied past a USC team ranked atop the coaches' poll and second by The Associated Press. But if that 24–23 win was the "greatest upset ever," how come the Bay Area wasn't abuzz afterward?

Sure, the Bay Area is more of a pro sports market than a college one, and, yes, some folks called in to sports-talk radio to relish one of Stanford's rare football triumphs. But then it was over, just like USC's unbeaten season.

You'd think the "greatest upset ever" would figure to have some staying power on people's tongues. Nah. This was Stanford football, and if you want proof of the Cardinal's popularity, consider that not one game was a sellout when Stanford opened up its rebuilt stadium in 2006. If this was the lone loss USC would suffer, then maybe that would enhance the "greatness" factor. But the Trojans also lost later that season to Oregon, and, hence, the diminished importance of an early season upset like Stanford-USC.

Stanford's win, however, did define "The Year of the Upsets." It started with Division I-AA Appalachian State winning at Michigan's "Big House." Half the Top 10 fell the following week, and soon thereafter was 36-point underdog Syracuse winning at Louisville. Actually, the year technically started with a terrific upset in January in the Sugar Bowl, when Boise State won in amazing fashion over Oklahoma.

Stanford's upset unfolded in dramatic fashion, capped by quarterback Tavita Pritchard's 10-yard touchdown pass to Mark Bradford on fourth-and-goal with 49 seconds remaining. Pritchard, the nephew of former Washington State star Jack Thompson, was making his first career start. Earlier on the winning drive, on fourth-and-20, Pritchard converted a 20-yard pass to Richard Sherman at the USC 9-yard line. A great footnote to the upset came when Pritchard revealed he couldn't hear his coach's play call on that fourth-and-20 so he went with his own play.

USC had a 35-game win streak going at the Coliseum and plenty of motivation entering the Stanford game. The Trojans had just slipped from number one to number two in the polls because of a narrow win over Washington State, and they had been baited during the offseason by new Stanford coach Jim Harbaugh, who dubbed the Trojans as college football's greatest team ever. Well, if that was the case, then maybe this was the greatest upset.

Two years earlier, the New York Times named Centre's 1921 win over Harvard as the biggest college football upset. Then, in 2006, ESPN compiled its own list, and atop it was Navy's 14–2 win over top-ranked Army in 1950. Second on ESPN's list was Notre Dame snapping second-ranked Oklahoma's 47-game win streak with a 7–0 win in 1957. Fast forward 50 years and there was Notre Dame getting upset by Navy, which subsequently cancelled classes the following Monday at the Naval Academy to celebrate its first win over the Irish in 44 years.

Measuring the "greatness" of upsets these days seems to coincide more with where the point spread was set, rather than if bragging rights or title hopes were at stake. That's why Stanford's upset conjured up memories of 1985 Oregon State (a 36-point underdog) topping Washington, and Temple (a 35-point underdog) knocking off Virginia Tech in 1998.

Each upset, of course, has its own special tale, such as Carnegie Tech's 1926 beating of fourth-ranked Notre Dame, which played without Coach Knute Rockne, who opted instead to attend the Army-Navy game. Don't forget about Slip Madigan's 1930 St. Mary's team taking the train cross country to stun Fordham 20–12.

So what tale could Harbaugh provide? Well, when the former NFL quarterback was hired to coach Stanford—located directly across the street from where he played for Palo Alto High School—Harbaugh said he would approach his job "with enthusiasm unknown to mankind." Sure enough, in his first season, he at least provided a degree of point-spread upset that hadn't been seen before in college football history. And at season's end, Stanford fans were celebrating again, knocking off Cal, and reclaiming The Axe trophy. That's the only upset that really matters on The Farm, so surely Stanford fans won't mind if we rule that their win over USC isn't the greatest upset in college football history. That honor should be reserved for those upsets that had more meaning in the late-season polls and drew more chatter across the nation, much less the Bay Area.

WHO'S THE MOST FAMOUS STANFORD SPORTS PRODUCT?

 Don't overthink this. Really. Stop. Okay, here's a hint: He's likely the most famous athlete in the world. That's right, Tiger Woods, a one-time accounting major on The Farm. He also dabbled in golf. And he got mugged on campus as a freshman. But that's not the story we're here to tell. No, Tiger deserves to be the top Cardinal because he's revolutionized golf, and he also put in two fine years at Stanford from 1995–96. He was a two-time All-American, a two-time Pac-10 player of the year, and he left Stanford after winning the NCAA's 1996 individual championship, having come in fifth the year before as a freshman.

Flip open Stanford's 2007 football media guide and, voila, there's a couple shots of Woods, including one page where he's the only athlete among the likes of prominent alumni such as Sandra Day O'Connor, Phil Knight, Reese Witherspoon, and Sally Ride.

Some may scoff at the selection of Woods in this debate. That's understandable. When you think of Tiger, you think of Augusta, St. Andrews, or Pebble Beach much more so than Stanford. So perhaps those in line for the throne are former Stanford quarterbacks Jim Plunkett (1970 Heisman winner, Rose Bowl champion, two-time Super Bowl winner with the Raiders) and John Elway (Stanford-record 77 career touchdown passes, two-time Super Bowl champ with the Denver Broncos).

Other familiar names in high-profile sports are John McEnroe (tennis), Tom Watson (golf), Mark Madsen (basketball), James Lofton (football), and John Lynch (football, but also a Stanford baseball player).

If you want to go old school, we suggest arguing the case of All-American fullback Ernie Nevers (1923–25), basketball sensation Hank Luisetti (introduced the one-handed shot in the 1930s), and Olympic decathlete Bob Mathias (also a Stanford football player in 1951–52). Other notable Olympians: Pablo Morales, Summer Sanders, Janet Evans, Eric Heiden, Kerri Strug, Debbi Thomas, Kerri Walsh, Julie Foudy, and Jennifer Azzi.

All of them, among other Stanford student athletes, deserve to be held in high esteem. But first on the tee is Tiger Woods. His dalliance with Stanford may have been brief, but it was memorable, and maybe those Stanford economic classes have helped him count all the money he's racked up in his remarkable career.

WHO IS CAL'S MOST FAMOUS SPORTS PRODUCT?

93 Jason Kidd played only two seasons for Cal basketball in the mid 1990s, but his legacy remains so strong, and his sport remains so popular, that he is currently the Bears' most famous athlete. That goes for recent past or present, actually.

Kidd was the local boy makes good. An Alameda product, he stayed home to spark Cal's basketball team to two NCAA Tournament runs. He put Cal back on the map after decades of futility, especially with a 1993 second-round upset of two-time defending national champion Duke.

Kidd parlayed his triple-double skills into a successful NBA career. That said, Cal has had more accomplished athletes come through the ranks, though just not as famous as Kidd. There was 1920s tennis product Helen Wills, who won eight Wimbledon and seven U.S. singles titles. Cal's had more than its share of Olympic champions, led by swimmers Matt Biondi (seven gold medals), as well as Natalie Coughlin and Mary T. Meagher, who also won multiple gold medals.

Cal's baseball program has produced major league MVPs in Jackie Jensen (1958, Red Sox) and Jeff Kent

(2000, Giants). The football program can tout Kansas City Chiefs tight end Tony Gonzalez, Green Bay Packers quarterback Aaron Rodgers, Raiders cornerback Nnamdi Asomugha, Buffalo Bills running back Marshawn Lynch, 1975 Heisman runner-up Chuck Muncie, and 1975 first overall NFL draft pick Steve Bartkowski. Other NBA-bound products besides Kidd include Kevin Johnson, Shareef Abdur-Raheem, Lamond Murray, Sean Lampley and, most recently, Leon Powe.

Unfortunately, one Cal alumn who can't hold up well in this debate is Jerry Mathers. You know, The Beaver. The problem is, Theodore Cleaver got a D in gym class in one episode. Oh well, Cal will always have The Kidd.

THE BAY AREA'S SPORTS SUBURBS

WHICH GREAT SHARK HAS BEEN THE GREATEST?

When the last-place San Jose Sharks traded for Joe Thornton on November 30, 2005, his arrival was trumpeted so much, it sounded like the Bay Area was getting Wayne Gretzky Lite. Sure enough, Thornton immediately lived up to the hype and became the first Shark to win the Hart Trophy as the NHL's MVP, in conjunction with the Art Ross Trophy as the league's scoring leader.

He's been a phenomenal offensive catalyst, dishing off assists like no one else. Actually, he joined Gretzky and Mario Lemieux as the only players to post consecutive 90-assist seasons, with Thornton doing so in his first two Sharks campaigns. A reliable presence in the lineup, Thornton spent his first seven seasons in Boston, and he warmed up so much to the Sharks, he gave them a home-town discount when he signed a contract extension in July 2007.

In December 2007, Thornton had a no-look, backhand assist to Patrick Marleau that could only have been more amazing had it come in the playoffs. He led the NHL in assists (67) in the 2007–08 season, and he led the Sharks in goals (29). His tremendous second-half surge helped the Sharks go 20 consecutive games without a loss in regulation. Then, in the first round of the playoffs, Thornton got credit for one of the most dramatic goals in Sharks history, with him tipping in Douglas Murray's slapshot in the final 10 seconds of a Game 4 win at Calgary.

From 1995–2003, in the pre-Thornton days, Owen Nolan owned the town. He may not match up to Thornton's talents, but Nolan carved a niche as one of the Sharks' most popular players, and most prolific scorers. Nolan helped the Sharks to five straight playoff appearances between 1998–2002. Nolan left town in 2003 (for Toronto) as the Sharks' all-time leading scorer, but that title's been snatched by Marleau, whose stock took a hit when he clammed up in the 2007 playoffs. When the next season arrived, though, Marleau was still wearing the captain's "C" on his sweater, and he broke out of a fog once the 2008 trade deadline passed with him remaining a Shark.

While Marleau might merit some consideration for the Shark with the best bite, so might Russian center Igor Larionov, whose sensational NHL career included a 1993–94 campaign with the resurgent Sharks. Goaltenders Evgeni Nabokov and Arturs Irbe have entrenched themselves in Sharks lore, and another guy who you shouldn't ignore is Jonathan Cheechoo, who became the first Shark to win the Rocket Richard Trophy when he tallied a franchise-record 56 goals in 2005–06. In February 2008, Cheechoo's ninth career hat trick gave Sharks coach Ron Wilson his 500th coaching win. Cheechoo, Wilson, and the rest of the Sharks owe much of their recent success to one guy, the guy who's the greatest Shark yet—Thornton.

HE SHOOTS, HE SCORES: THE SHARKS' BEST GOAL?

95 Owen Nolan had already scored two goals in the 1997 All-Star Game on San Jose's home ice when, to the delight of Sharks' fans, he called his shot and completed his hat trick.

Nolan tracked down a loose puck at the blue line, skated ahead three strides, and then motioned with his right hand toward the upper-right corner of the net. That's just where he blistered his shot in a one-on-one opportunity against Eastern Conference goalie Dominik Hasek. Fans celebrated by tossing their hats on to the ice below, never mind that the Western Conference trailed 11–7 with about two minutes remaining.

While Nolan's goal has a sentimental spot in Sharks' fans hearts, it came with him in a purple all-star sweater. Thus, let's find the best goal by a man in teal.

The Sharks have had more than their share of playoff struggles since their 1991–92 birth. But there have also been thrilling shots, three of which resulted in playoff-series clinchers.

On May 19, 1995, Ray Whitney provided an epic chapter in Sharks lore. His goal in double overtime lifted the seventh-seeded Sharks past the host Calgary Flames 5–4 in Game 7 of their first-round playoff series.

Five years later, the Sharks won another first-round series in Game 7 fashion, and it was Owen Nolan's 75-foot slap shot that changed the course of their 3–1 win at St. Louis. Nolan's goal came with 10.2 seconds remaining in the first period, and while it gave the Sharks a 2–0 lead, it also deflated the Kiel Center crowd.

But the best of the bunch is Jamie Baker's Game 7 winner over the top-seeded Detroit Red Wings on April 30, 1994. It was the Sharks' first-ever foray into the playoffs, and they immediately made history by becoming the first number eight seed to dispatch a number one. It was a season that marked the Sharks' move from San Francisco's Cow Palace into a new arena that revitalized downtown San Jose. It was a season that started 0–8–1, and one that wasn't ready to end against the Red Wings. Baker's shot past Chris Osgood assured that, though the Sharks still had 13 minutes to burn before the series was theirs.

The Sharks took their next opponents to seven games, as well, only to fall to the Toronto Maple Leafs. But a down-town parade and rally still attracted a ton of teal supporters. All those goals will pale in comparison to whichever one puts the Sharks into their first Stanley Cup Finals, or, dare we dream further, whichever one gives them their first NHL championship.

WHO'S THE BAY AREA'S MOST FAMOUS FEMALE ATHLETE?

96 A jubilant Brandi Chastain stripped off her jersey, exposed her black sports bra to the world and everyone took notice. Of her. Of women's soccer. And of sports bras, of course. Chastain's signature moment was a watershed moment not just in her career, but all of women's athletics. The whole nation caught soccer fever during the United States' inspiring run to the 1999 Women's World Cup title, which Chastain delivered with her goal in an epic shootout against China before 90,125 fans at Pasadena's Rose Bowl.

So did that moment still resonate and make her the Bay Area's most famous female athlete?

Another famous female from the Bay is ice skater Kristi Yamaguchi, a Fremont native and the 1992 Olympic gold medallist. Her fame surely reached another demographic during the spring of 2008 when she participated in ABC's Dancing with the Stars. Another skating diva from here was Peggy Fleming, who won Olympic gold in 1968.

And whenever the Summer Olympics come around, it's a good bet the Bay Area will have a swimming sensation, such as those in past Games with Mary T. Meagher (or, "Madam

Butterfly"), Natalie Coughlin, Janet Evans, Summer Sanders, Jenny Thompson, and Anne Warner Cribbs.

Stanford's Jennifer Azzi brought championship women's basketball to the Bay Area's forefront, as she led the Cardinal to its first NCAA title in 1990. She also won Olympic gold in Atlanta and spent some of her pro career with the San Jose Lasers of the now defunct ABL.

Stanford is where one of the world's most famous female athletes descended in the fall of 2007. But teenage golfer Michelle Wie came to study, not play for the Cardinal, having turned pro in 2005 and already competed on both the PGA and LPGA tours. One Bay Area-bred golfer who's already rocketing to stardom is Pleasanton's Paula Creamer. She's got a ways to go, though, to catch up to LPGA Hall of Famer Julie Inkster, a Santa Cruz native and San Jose State product.

One of the Bay Area's all-time greats, and one who's been too forgotten, is Berkeley tennis phenom Helen Wills (Moody Roark). She was her generation's Williams sisters. Actually, she was better. At age 17, she won the first of seven U.S. Championships, and 15 years later, she won her eighth and final Wimbledon. If "Miss Poker Face" was doing that today, she'd be as famous as anyone.

But as famous as Chastain? Remember that whirlwind of patriotism in 1999, and what ensued after her Women's World Cup winner? She received the most, um, exposure after her bra-baring celebration. Magazine covers, television commercials, late-night talk shows, and an eventual ESPN sideline reporting gig. Her goal—and her unbridled enthusiasm afterward—made her an instant icon in her sport, and she's continued as a spokeswoman not just for soccer, but all of women's athletics. The Bay Area is a soccer hotbed and Chastain is its top role model, having played at San Jose's Archbishop Mitty High School and Santa Clara University.

Thus, Chastain is the First Lady of Bay Area sports. For the record, when told she won this debate, she did not rip off her blouse and celebrate. She must be waiting for the medal ceremony.

WHAT WERE THE BAY AREA'S TOP GOLF MOMENTS?

 97 Whenever PGA, LPGA, and Senior PGA golfers make annual stops in the Bay Area, their sport is able to steal headlines in this crowded sports marketplace. It's a tradition: decades ago, golf dominated the headlines, especially San Francisco's City Championship. So what are the greatest hits? Because Pebble Beach is over an hour drive from the South Bay, we'll reserve its golf tales for another debate. Here are moments that make up the Bay Area's ultimate par-five:

5. TIGER VS. DALY, 2005 AMEX:

Classic John Daly drama unfolded in 2005 at Harding Park, where he missed a three-foot putt on the second playoff hole to give Tiger Woods the American Express Championship. Daly lost more that night, dropping $1.6 million in Las Vegas slot machines, or so he wrote in his autobiography.

4. KEN VENTURI, 1964 U.S. OPEN:

Eight years after winning his third City Championship in his native San Francisco, Venturi's career came back strong with his 1964 triumph in the U.S. Open at Congressional in

Washington D.C. He overcame dehydration and heat exhaustion to claim the win as well as Sports Illustrated's Sportsman of the Year honor.

3. LEE JANZEN, 1998 U.S. OPEN:

Janzen not only came from seven strokes down to overtake Payne Stewart, but what made this triumph special was a certain tee shot into a cypress tree at Olympic. Janzen's errant drive on the fifth hole landed in that tree, and as he headed back to the tee to hit another drive, wind blew his ball out of the tree, and Janzen later chipped in to save par on the fifth.

2. JOHNNY MILLER, 1973 U.S. OPEN:

This championship didn't take place in the Bay Area, but rather at Oakmont (Pa.) Country Club, where San Francisco's Miller posted an 8-under 63 on the final day to win the Open. Miller, who shot a 76 the previous day, went on to win the 1976 British Open, and three AT&T Pebble Beach National Pro-Am titles.

1. JACK FLECK, 1955 U.S. OPEN

Ben Hogan's quest for an unprecedented fifth U.S. Open crown was denied by a then-unknown Fleck at San Francisco's Olympic Club. Fleck birdied the 72nd hole and beat Hogan in an 18-hole playoff the following day, with Fleck shooting a 69, and Hogan a 72 in one of sports' all-time upsets.

Honorable mention: Before Tony Lema died tragically at age 32 in a 1966 plane crash, he was one of America's hottest golfers, highlighted by his 1964 British Open win at St. Andrews....San Francisco native George Archer's lengthy career was highlighted by his win at the 1969 Masters, finishing a stroke ahead of Billy Casper, George Knudson, and Tom Weiskopf....In three other Olympic Club classics, Scott Simpson edged Tom Watson by a stroke in the 1987 U.S. Open, Billy Casper rallied past Arnold Palmer in the 1966 U.S. Open, and Nathaniel Crosby (Bing's son) won the 1981 U.S. Amateur.

WHAT WERE PEBBLE BEACH'S BEST MOMENTS?

One of the most picturesque places in the world has showcased many epic moments in golf, from the Crosby Clambake (now the AT&T Pebble Beach National Pro-Am) to the U.S. Open, and amateurs. Here are Pebble Beach's top-five moments (and, we must warn you, they don't include the priceless scenes of Jack Lemmon or Bill Murray in the Pro-Am):

5. TOM KITE, 1992 U.S. OPEN

Chipping in at the seventh hole set Kite on his way to his first and only U.S. Open title. Kite won by two strokes, and he still considers that lob wedge for birdie the best shot of his career.

4. HALE IRWIN, 1984 AT&T

Trailing by a stroke, Irwin sent his 18th-hole tee shot toward the rocky ocean shore, where it ricocheted off rocks and into the fairway. Irwin made a birdie on the 18th and forced a playoff that he won against Jim Nelford.

3. JACK NICKLAUS, 1972 U.S. OPEN

Yes, 10 years before he would lose the Open here to Watson, Nicklaus also had his own 17th-hole miracle. The "Golden Bear" in the yellow sweater blistered a one-iron, his drive took one-hop off the flagstick, and he tapped in for birdie en route to his third U.S. Open title.

2. TIGER WOODS, 2000 U.S. OPEN

After rallying to win the AT&T Pro-Am for his sixth straight tour victory, Woods returned to Pebble four months later for an amazing encore. He won his first U.S. Open by a mere 15 strokes, posting scores of 65, 69, 71, and a bogey-free 67 for a combined total of 272, tying the record for lowest 72-hole score in a U.S. Open.

1. TOM WATSON, 1982 U.S. OPEN

Close your eyes, envision Pebble Beach's par-3 17th with the Pacific Ocean as the backdrop. You can still see Tom Watson standing between two bunkers in the left rough, chipping with a sand wedge and his ball dropping into the hole for an incredible birdie. Watson, in his blue Fila sweater, didn't produce a fist pump but rather a short victory lap with his head held high in pure glee. For good measure, he birdied the 18th to defeat Jack Nicklaus by two strokes.

IS NASCAR WEEKEND NORTHERN CALIFORNIA'S BIGGEST SPORTING EVENT?

99 Okay, before you start protesting over what constitutes "biggest" event, let's define it as thus: Big crowd, big stars, big stakes, and it all keeps getting bigger and bigger. Infineon Raceway becomes a racing fan's Mecca for at least one weekend each summer when NASCAR rolls into the Sonoma hills for the Toyota/Save Mart 350.

What, NASCAR is a niche sport? Hey, so is golf, and even though Pebble Beach offers a phenomenal and spiritual setting for the AT&T National Pro-Am, ticket sales are capped at 35,000 each day. More fans actually invade the Monterey Peninsula for motorcycle races at Laguna Seca. While much of the AT&T golf crowd reflects that sports' upper-class mentality, NASCAR weekend brings in over 100,000 fans with a diverse blend of stereotypical rednecks, corporate honks, and true racing followers.

Before we further compare NASCAR to AT&T golf, let's just knock out any arguments you might have in favor of other sports.

Opening Day in baseball is always special, and the Giants and A's have had some excellent seasons of late, but you're not going to have thousands of fans camping out for days in motorhomes before the first pitch. As wildly popular as the NFL is, do you really think 100,000 fans would show up for a 49ers or Raiders game, even if they somehow made the playoffs ever again? Whereas other locales might have a January college football bowl game to rally around, the Bay Area doesn't. The "Big Game" between Cal and Stanford rarely unfolds with postseason bids on the line for both teams, while the Emerald Bowl usually brings in lower-tier teams to AT&T Park in December.

Okay, back to NASCAR vs. AT&T golf. Top drivers aren't skipping Sonoma's road course, unlike the increasing amount of top golfers (See: Tiger Woods) who bypass Pebble Beach because of its long rounds, bumpy greens, and sometime nasty weather. Pebble does get the nod for more picturesque views, and fans there can get more exercise walking the fairways. But you can't get fried turkey legs out on the links like you can at the NASCAR tracks.

NASCAR fans are a rabid bunch who worship the Sprint Cup series' lone Northern California stop. Infineon's 12-turn course is unique, and while NASCAR fans get to cheer for their sports' regulars, road-race fans also get their thirst quenched.

Infineon also offers up a native son to cheer for, as Jeff Gordon grew up in Vallejo before moving to Indiana as a teenager to accelerate his career. When Gordon won for the fifth time in 2006, it came on the same weekend he was inducted into Infineon's Wall of Fame.

If you're looking for a great seat, head to Turn 9, but get to the track early to truly experience the biggest weekend in Northern California sports.

WHAT WAS THE BAY AREA'S BEST YEAR IN SPORTS?

100 While the Bay Area was mired in more terrible football from the 49ers and Raiders in November 2007, the San Francisco Chronicle noted how the year wasn't a total loss for the local sports scene and decided to rank it among the top 10 in Bay Area history. Yes, confetti did fall earlier in the year, both during Barry Bonds' passing of Hank Aaron on the home-run chart as well as the Warriors' return to the NBA playoffs after a 12-year absence. But 2007 won't be remembered as the top year, not when the 49ers and Raiders combined for a 9–23 record.

Let's start our investigation with 1982. Ten days into that storybook year, the 49ers' produced the play—or, The Catch—that launched the franchise's dynasty of five Super Bowls. Dwight Clark's last-minute touchdown catch of Joe Montana's high pass into the back of Candlestick Park's north end zone lifted the 49ers past the rival Dallas Cowboys 28–27. Two weeks later, third-year coach Bill Walsh delivered the 49ers their first Lombardi trophy.

The Giants couldn't answer with a pennant that summer, but they did provide the next sweetest thing—denying the hated Los Angeles Dodgers a chance to win the National League West. A day after the Giants were eliminated from pennant contention, Joe Morgan lined a three-run, seventh-inning homer to topple the Dodgers and foil their plans for a one-game playoff against the Atlanta Braves.

As if those magical moments weren't enough, the Bay Area became the center of the sports universe on November 20. That's the birthday of The Play, Cal's five-lateral kickoff return for a band-bashing touchdown in the final four seconds of their Big Game triumph over Stanford and senior quarterback John Elway.

Another special year was 1989, which started with the 49ers' Super Bowl XXIII comeback against the Cincinnati Bengals. Montana capped the winning 92-yard drive with a touchdown to John Taylor with 34 seconds remaining, giving the 49ers' their second straight Lombardi Trophy and fourth in eight years.

Unlike in 1982, the Giants successfully answered the 49ers' exploits by winning a National League West pennant in 1989. Those Giants then went on to their first World Series since 1962, with Will Clark delivering a clutch two-out, two-run single in the Game 5-clinching win over the Chicago Cubs in the NLCS.

But the Giants' run literally came to a screeching halt in the World Series, where a 7.1-magnitude earthquake struck about 30 minutes before Game 3 at Candlestick. The cross-bay A's went on to sweep the World Series, and even though it was the Battle of the Bay, the earthquake took the luster off that convergence of Bay Area teams, not to mention the overall vibe of the 1989 sports year.

That was the A's first World Series title since 1974, another year which arguably was among the Bay Area's best. The A's won their third straight World Series title by taking Game 5 from the Los Angeles Dodgers. Joe Rudi's seventh-inning homer put the A's ahead in that Game 5, and they protected their cushion an inning later when Bill Buckner got thrown out at third base on a perfect relay from Reggie Jackson to Dick Green to Sal Bando.

A month later on that 1974 calendar, Stanford won the Big Game on Mike Langford's 50-yard field goal as time expired. It was Steve Bartkowski's final game before being selected as the NFL draft's first overall pick in 1975.

Before 1974 was done, the Raiders delivered one of the most exciting playoff games ever, winning the "Sea of Hands" game against the vaunted Miami Dolphins. That thrilling comeback was capped off by Clarence Davis' touchdown catch with 24 seconds remaining, Davis fishing his way through the hands of Dolphins defenders to nab Ken Stabler's pass for the 28–26 triumph.

Want more years to consider? Let's do a condensed list: 1959 (Cal basketball wins the NCAA tourney after its football team reaches the Rose Bowl), 1968 (A's Catfish Hunter throws perfect game, the Giants' Gaylord Perry hurls no-hitter), 1972 (A's win first World Series title,

Raiders endure Immaculate Reception), 1993 (Santa Clara and Cal enjoy March Madness upsets), 1997 (Brian Johnson homers vs. the Dodgers), and 2002 (Tuck Rule dooms the Raiders, Scott Hatteberg's homer gives the A's their 20th straight win).

So which year is our favorite? If you appreciate the 49ers' dynasty, hate the Dodgers, and love the Cal-Stanford rivalry, then you'll agree with us that 1982 is the greatest year in Bay Area sports lore.

Of course, after making it through all of the previous 99 arguments, you may decide that 2008 was the greatest year because that's when this book landed in your hands. Or not. Hmmn, perhaps that could be our 101st debate.

INDEX
by Subject

295

INDEX
by Name

299

Photo by Brad Mangin

Cam Inman is a sports columnist with the Bay Area News Group and has worked with the *Contra Costa Times* since 1995. He's a Bay Area native who grew up in Cupertino and turned pro as a sportswriter at age sixteen. Twenty years later, he's still covering the Bay Area sports scene with the zest of a teenager. He's covered five Super Bowls for the *Times* since 2002, he's served as a 49ers correspondent for the *Sporting News*, and he appears frequently on CBS's San Francisco affiliate, KPIX. Hobbies include 16-handicap golf, pushing a jogger stroller in the Pleasanton Father's Day 10K, and making endless trips to the hardware store. He lives in Pleasanton with his wife, Jennifer Branchini, and their three children, Kate, Brooke, and Grant. He once had a dog named Max, the subject of his first published story, in fifth grade (ghost authored by his mother, Irene).